3 3020 01105 3336

D0743607

MEET THE CANDIDATES 2020

PETE BUTTIGIEG

PETE BUTTIGIEG

A VOTER'S GUIDE

Series Edited by
SCOTT DWORKIN

Compiled and Written by Grant Stern

Skyhorse Publishing

Skyhorse Publishing books may be purchased in bulk at special discounts for
sales promotion, corporate gifts, fund-raising, or educational purposes. Special
editions can also be created to specifications. For details, contact the Special Sales
Department, Skyhorse Publishing, 307 West 36th Street, 11th Floor, New York,
NY 10018 or info@skyhorsepublishing.com.

Skyhorse® and Skyhorse Publishing® are registered trademarks of Skyhorse
Publishing, Inc.®, a Delaware corporation.

Visit our website at www.skyhorsepublishing.com.

10 9 8 7 6 5 4 3 2 1

Library of Congress Cataloging-in-Publication Data is available on file.

Cover design by Brian Peterson

ISBN: 978-1-5107-5241-2
Ebook ISBN: 978-1-5107-5242-9

Printed in the United States of America

CONTENTS

PETE
BUTTIGIEG

INTRODUCTION TO PETE BUTTIGIEG

BY SERIES EDITOR SCOTT DWORKIN

When South Bend's mayor, Pete Buttigieg, launched his exploratory committee for president on January 23, 2019, not many folks thought he would actually have a chance of winning any primary, let alone becoming the Democratic nominee. But since then, Buttigieg's popularity has skyrocketed, turning his underdog campaign into a formidable candidacy. He's pieced together a stellar campaign team, a list of some solid endorsements, and has been able to positively stay in the news at a steady pace since the beginning.

A major reason why Buttigieg has broken out in to the top five in the pack is due to his commonsense rhetoric which resonates with folks across the country. You can see this in his campaign slogan, "A Fresh Start For America," a line that is sure to hook a lot of Americans facing the turmoil of the Trump presidency.

Buttigieg's policies are not clearly listed on his website, but many of the Democratic candidates' platforms aren't on their sites, either. It is tough to assess his vision, though, without knowing where he stands on a lot of different issues. Of the top five polled 2020 Democratic primary candidates, the leader—Vice President Biden—has no published agenda yet, either, while the three senators that are candidates have extensive bodies of policy either on their campaign websites or in the bills they've introduced over the past year. But Buttigieg's announcement speech and recent press articles do finally reveal a robust, progressive policy platform from the mayor. More of that is detailed in Chapter 4.

The mayor's policy stances, we discovered, are clearly progressive. But more important, he makes decisions and presents issues in a way that understands and speaks to the real, everyday concerns of the average American. That makes him a candidate to watch.

Although that platform doesn't set him apart from the pack, there are a lot of different things that do. And it's not just his ability to connect with voters. Buttigieg's age, thirty-seven, is both helpful and hurtful to his candidacy. Some younger voters have found him appealing, as he can connect easier with millennials then some of the candidates in their seventies. But I've also heard several voters downplay his candidacy due to his age, saying things along the lines of, "He is young, he has a bright future, but his time isn't now."

It is mind-bending, though, and hilarious, when he reminds us that he will be Trump's age in 2054.

Another thing that sets the mayor apart from the other candidates is his military service. He served in the U.S. Navy Reserve from 2009 to 2017, and was deployed to Afghanistan (by request) for seven months. Most of the other folks in the running have never served in the military, so this unique background will give him the opportunity to separate himself from the rest.

Another positive for the Buttigieg campaign is the fact he hasn't spent much time in DC, so he is able to say he's an outsider who is looking to change things up. Almost all of the other Democratic candidates have spent years in elected federal office, based in DC. This really does separate him from the mix, and voters and donors are starting to take notice.

All of these experiences will likely benefit his candidacy more than not. Buttigieg is clearly a leader who is mature, has poise, and has a unique ability to be diplomatic yet strike back fiercely when needed. He is smart and quick-witted, and does not take criticism lying down.

If Buttigieg were to become president, he would be a strong, pragmatic leader. He would definitely reach across the aisle and look to accomplish as much as he can in a bipartisan fashion. He would never tweet nonsense, and would not violate the Constitution. He would honor our country and understand the great responsibility in being Commander-in-Chief.

We've seen this to be true in a few examples of how Buttigieg has handled divisive issues and situations in the past.

One of them happened while serving as mayor in April of 2018, where he had to make a tough call about the abortion debate, a significantly divisive issue in the conservative state of Indiana. He had to decide whether or not an antiabortion group should be able to take up a commercial space next to a women's health and abortion clinic.[1] Buttigieg took the bold step of vetoing his city council's decision that would've allowed the move. But to defuse the situation, he made the following statement: "I don't think it would be responsible to situate two groups, literally right next to each other, in a neighborhood, that have diametrically opposed views on the most divisive social issue of our time."

Even though he knew some would find it unpopular, he still made a clear decision on what he believed was best, and safest, for his city. Buttigieg even cited statistics that said a community was three times as likely to experience violent acts or harassment if an abortion clinic is situated next to an antiabortion center. That is a staggering number. He embraced a scientific study and used those numbers to help explain why he made the decision. To cap it off, he said: "Issues on the legality or morality of abortion are dramatically beyond my paygrade as a mayor." The bottom line is that he made it about the security of his city, not about the issue of abortion. That made it much less controversial, and simmered down the opposition's argument.

He obviously did his homework, and didn't just rely on public sentiment, which is brave in itself. But this kind of move is presidential.

It takes courage to make strong decisions that might be unpopular or would welcome a clear negative response, especially in politics. It shows the mayor is wise and able to play the political chess needed at the presidential level, where every move you make matters and every word you use is scrutinized. He took some blowback, but in the end it was clear to most of the people in his community that he had made the sensible choice.

Another divisive issue that Buttigieg has handled masterfully in the past is that of LGBTQ rights. As the first Democratic candidate to run as an openly gay man, Buttigieg not only makes his stance abundantly clear on equal rights for members of every gender identity and sexual orientation, but sees his candidacy as an instrument for change, whether he wins the nomination or not. The mayor said this to LGBTQ newspaper the *Washington Blade*: "Actually having someone from the LGBTQ community on the ballot is important. It will make things better for the next person who comes along and that America needs to be given a chance to demonstrate that it's ready for this."[2]

Buttigieg also stood vehemently against Trump's transgender military ban. And given Buttigieg's military experience, he possesses a very unique view of how little it matters if someone is transgender or not in the military. The mayor makes a great point. If you can do your job, all that matters is the fact it's a fellow American next to you. Nothing else.

The key point here is that Buttigieg doesn't let issues that normally split the electorate get used to divide people on party lines. He doesn't make it about partisanship. He makes it about common sense. Buttigieg has a real talent for conveying a clear message to the masses and, more importantly, for governing and speaking with the best interests of the common American in mind. And that is how a true leader can unify our divided country.

He's unique, he's thoughtful, decent, and charismatic. And it shows on the campaign trail. He already has displayed how knowledgeable he is of almost every major issue. He's smart, well spoken, and doesn't seem to get rattled easily. He's confronted protesters and hecklers without pause, and has been able to push back against continuous attacks from people on the national stage like Vice President Mike Pence. These are just some of the reasons why the mayor's campaign has started to take off.

And the momentum is starting to show, as he started to gain in the polls and even raised a surprising $7 million in the first few months of the campaign.[3] He even started to lock down fund-raisers with major donors who were backing candidates like Senator Kamala Harris. The fact they are now splitting the difference with other candidates is a testament to the fact that they see a future in Mayor Pete. Several donors have told me personally that no matter if it is "Kamala-Pete or Pete-Kamala," they think of it as a winning ticket.

The Buttigieg campaign has also received some surprising endorsements including those of Rep. Don Beyer (D-VA), former Chairman of the Democratic National Committee Steve Grossman, the mayors of Austin, Texas, West Sacramento, California and Dayton, Ohio. In addition, he's been endorsed by five former ambassadors, state senator Michael Rodrigues from Massachusetts, and Cole Reel, a state representative in New Hampshire.[4]

Yet, there are several negatives surrounding Buttigieg that will start to be amplified as we get closer to the primary season.

One of those negatives is the lack of political experience when compared to other candidates. In the past, less political experience usually would be something that is conveyed as a positive, but not as much in 2020. People will want someone who has experience legislating, or at least a clear vision to move America forward. We learned via Trump that inexperience in government can be a very bad thing for our country.

An additional growing problem as the mayor's campaign expands is the fact his ties to big money are expanding with it.[5] He's started to have private fund-raising events hosted with supporters linked to billionaires, something some of his primary opponents like Warren have pledged not to do.[6] But money is still a necessary evil in politics. And since Buttigieg hasn't been a federally elected candidate for years, he needs money in order to run a real campaign. As long as he doesn't become beholden to the donors who give to him, it will turn out to be much more positive than negative.

Another issue Buttigieg is likely to be confronted with is his stance against free college. He said this while speaking to a group of college kids in April of 2019: "Americans who have a college degree earn more than Americans who don't. As a progressive, I have a hard time getting my head around the idea a majority who earn less because they didn't go to college subsidize a minority who earn more because they did."[7]

That makes a lot of sense to some folks. But it still will open him up to criticism on the campaign trail from progressives like Warren, who are making it a key part of their campaign.

A big red flag that we spotted when looking further into Buttigieg's record is the fact he has pushed the statement "all lives matter" in the past. As a reminder, the "all lives matter" campaign was a counterargument against the Black Lives Matter movement. So this could become a major issue when it comes to approaching the African American vote.

Another thing people have been critical of is Buttigieg's support for a mandatory year of national service. "One thing we could do," says the military veteran who served in a war zone during his term of office, "would be to make it, if not legally obligatory, then certainly a social norm that anybody after they're eighteen spends a year in national service." He believes that it's "one of the ideas that everybody likes," but that will likely be challenged on the campaign trail.[8]

Recently, he has received a lot of criticism for the idea. If he changed it from mandatory to a situation where Americans can benefit from a year of service like getting a free education or some other incentive, then it would resonate more.

So there are some kinks he has to work out. And although he's had some miscues, and has made some ill-advised statements in the past, overall the Pete for America campaign platform is extremely progressive. It aligns with most other candidates in the race, but how he presents it separates him from the pack. He can go in depth with almost any issue, and he actually is knowledgeable of the fine print. Buttigieg is quick-witted and savvy when it comes to most issues. And he has a commanding presence in a room that looks presidential.

But can Mayor Pete Buttigieg win the Democratic primary? Yes, but it's going to be tough.

The pathway to victory is narrow, but it's still doable. With a mix of hard work and luck, he might be able to pull it off.

Former Vice President Biden's entry into the race for president makes things much more complicated for Buttigieg. It will make getting more endorsements and raising more money that much harder. As the Democratic field expands to over twenty candidates, it really makes it harder for any candidate to stand out and be heard among such a strong field of experienced politicians, some of whom have been spending years laying the groundwork for a presidential run, such as Senators Sanders, Warren, Harris, and the former vice president. Of course, the flip side of that is since he has already stood out early, he won't have that problem going forward now that Buttigieg has improbably become a household name. Or at least "Boot-Edge-Edge" has.

In order for Buttigieg to win the primary he probably would need to be able to pull out some wins before Super Tuesday, with, at a minimum, a top three finish in Iowa, New Hampshire, and South Carolina. He would also need endorsements from some of the groups that likely will support Biden, Booker, Harris, Sanders, or Warren. That'll be a tough sell, with it being so easy for groups not to endorse until there is a Democratic nominee. Some groups might talk about how they've had an allegiance with a candidate for years, so even if they don't endorse, their support is clearly already aligned with one of the candidates. President Obama indeed faced the same sort of challenges, but it wasn't such a vast field of candidates back in 2008.

If Buttigieg gains the necessary financial resources and is able to pull more endorsements from elected officials, labor unions, and progressive organizations, then he might have a clear path to the nomination. But again, that could become nearly impossible with the entry of former Vice President Biden into the mix.

One thing is certain about Buttigieg's candidacy: he is here to stay. It looks like he has already raised enough money to make it to Super Tuesday. And based on his national exposure to date, he will be a force to be reckoned with in the primary debates.

If Buttigieg is lucky enough to make it through the gauntlet of the Democratic primary process as the victor, he will then have to face the most cutthroat and corrupt campaigner in American history: President Donald Trump.

Trump is already starting with his line of attack against Buttigieg. In early May, Trump compared his looks to the old face from the cover of *Mad* magazine, saying: "Alfred E. Neuman cannot become president of the United States."[9] This is the first indication that Trump deems Buttigieg to be a genuine threat. As we've learned, Trump only attacks folks who threaten him. But in Mayor Pete fashion, he struck back with two jabs by saying: "I'll be honest. I had to Google that. I guess it's just a generational thing. I didn't get the reference. It's kind of funny, I guess. But he's also the president of the United States, and I'm surprised he's not spending more time trying to salvage this China deal."[10] Ouch.

In a general election matchup between Trump and Buttigieg, it would be difficult for Trump, that's for sure. With Buttigieg's background of growing up in the Midwest and his ability to talk to the voters that Hillary couldn't, it is completely possible that Pete could beat Trump in 2020. If they were to face off, I believe that Buttigieg would mop the floor with Trump. And that Pete would win states that Hillary didn't, including Iowa, Michigan, Ohio, North Carolina, Pennsylvania, and Wisconsin. If that's the outcome, Buttigieg would receive 317 electoral votes and Trump would receive 221.

So can Buttigieg win if he is the Democratic nominee? Absolutely.

As his campaign website grandly proclaims, "Our country needs a fresh start," adding "Pete stands for the better America that we know we can be."[11] If Democratic primary voters nominate Mayor Pete, he would probably beat Trump. And our country might get the "fresh start" he talks about.

WHO IS PETE BUTTIGIEG?

Mayor Pete Buttigieg's candidacy is a three-legged stool that rests upon his youth, his intellectual clarity of vision, and the insight he gained from his unique life experiences including military service, the Ivy League, and the world of business consulting. He declared his presidential exploratory committee on January 23, 2019, just days after releasing a memoir about his life.

Pete Buttigieg's seven-year record in public office is spread across thousands of local stories in the *South Bend Tribune*. Buttigieg came out in a letter to the editor in 2015, two months after the state's Republican governor passed sweeping antigay legislation that caused a national uproar and thrust the mayor into the political spotlight. Vice President Mike Pence was that governor, and he quickly rolled back Indiana's Religious Freedom Restoration Act after boycotts and public pressure.[1]

In the early part of the 2020 Democratic primary race, Pete Buttigieg turned Pence into his top political foil at a televised CNN Town Hall on March 10, 2019. His public shaming of the vice president by judging his actions against Pence's professed religious beliefs sparked a discussion about the role of faith in modern politics.

The next day, his campaign had a six-figure fund-raising haul, and his candidacy took off from there. Although, while it appeared that success solely sprung from his TV appearance, the campaign's work behind the scenes is what really leveraged the mayor's national exposure.

Pete Buttigieg aims his candidacy squarely at millennials, and at attracting the Midwestern voters who helped put President Obama in office by a landslide in 2008, but abandoned the Democratic nominee in 2016. His book *Shortest Way Home: One Mayor's Challenge and a Model for America's Future* begins with a history of the factory closures in his beloved hometown of South Bend, explaining the postindustrial city he grew up in as it turned into a college town. Unlike his competitors, Mayor Pete didn't employ a coauthor. The book became a *New York Times* best seller.[2]

Pete Buttigieg's campaign publishes its policy agenda in mid-May 2019. It centers around three concepts: Freedom, Security and Democracy. In all, his issues outline lists twenty-seven different issues under those categories ranging from the freedom not to have to choose between health care and financial survival to security, meaning that America has common-sense gun laws. However, it only contains a single paragraph on foreign policy, an important presidential portfolio.

Pete Buttigieg is a Harvard College grad and Rhodes Scholar who preferred going home, while simultaneously becoming a citizen of the world working for America's top management consulting firm McKinsey & Company. He quit that high-paying job to join the US Navy Reserve and run for a low-paying public service job in statewide elected office, which he lost. But he parlayed that political experience into a victory which landed him in the mayor's office of South Bend at the age of twenty-nine. The decline of his rust-belt hometown in Indiana started in the 1960s when

Studebaker shut down, and the city is best known as the home of Notre Dame University. The citizens of South Bend call him Mayor Pete.

The mayor's unique experience as a naval intelligence officer deployed to an active war zone in Afghanistan—while he was serving as mayor—confers upon him a credential that the incumbent president doesn't have. In fact, Buttigieg's limited résumé significantly surpasses President Trump's nonextant record of government experience outside of holding the nation's highest office. It's one of his campaign's pegs. In relation to the Democratic primary field, only two other Democratic candidates have military experience: Reps. Tulsi Gabbard (D-HI) and Seth Moulton (D-MA). Neither is drawing over 1 percent of voters as of May 2019 in aggregate polling.[3]

He is the first major candidate from either party to be openly gay and married to a same-sex spouse. It's a fact that doesn't define the mayor's campaign, but it is an important part of his story and his eventual rise to national political fame before embarking on a quixotic presidential campaign that suddenly became a leading effort in the 2020 Democratic primary. A *Time* magazine cover story told his husband's story; it wasn't bombshell news, but it reveals a personal side of the mayor that didn't even exist until a few short years ago.

"In so many ways, South Bend *is* our message," says Buttigieg frequently, and while his initiatives there achieved varying degrees of success, they represent the first major improvements to the city in decades.[4] Buttigieg's revitalization of its downtown areas is a huge step forward. His initiative to get rid of a thousand vacant homes in a thousand days was a success, though it had detractors. Mayor Pete's sensible plan to turn South Bend's old Studebaker factory into an innovation center is ongoing. The mayor's statements about policing and handling of his police department are going to come under close scrutiny.

In January 2017, the mayor mounted a campaign to be the new DNC chairperson and made a real splash in the race, gaining the kinds of endorsements that have recently turned into key campaign donors. His donors included a couple of former national Democratic Party chairs and two senators. Though his campaign wasn't successful, he made an impression in the national political scene with his ability to command media attention.

South Bend's residents appear to overwhelmingly support their mayor's bid for the presidency as it draws him away from his duties as a lame duck, which he manages remotely. He announced that he would not run for reelection in 2019, and his likely successor will be chosen in the city's Democratic primary by May 7th, since the city's voters are solidly blue.

In a twenty-one-person field as of May 2, 2019, Buttigieg is the youngest candidate at the age of thirty-seven. The constitutional minimum age for the job is thirty-five. If elected president, he would handily break the record Teddy Roosevelt holds for being the youngest president of the United States by four years. Kennedy was the youngest person to be elected to the job after his term as Massachusetts senator, when he was forty-three.

The mayor reasons that older candidates will not be around to see the results of their policies, but he will. However, he will have to overcome the real-world political issue that older voters participate in elections in droves and young voters are reliably unreliable the younger they get. But there's no denying that his candidacy and ideas resonate highly with the millennial generation voters who are sick of watching their elders in the baby boom generation dominate political discourse, and are upset over their rejection of President Obama, who Buttigieg once campaigned for.

On Mayor Pete's side is a suddenly massive following on social media. His audience is engaging with him at rates that rank him in the top five of the twenty-two person field for the month of April 2019, according to CrowdTangle data. A Quinnipiac University poll in early May 2019 placed him fourth in the race nationally, giving heartening news that voters believe that his sexuality is not an electability issue but sobering news about overall opinions on his chances in the race.[5]

He's not the only mayor in the race, though by far his campaign is outpacing those of other mayors thus far. Buttigieg's success may have inadvertently encouraged New York City's Mayor Bill de Blasio to jump into the race, which could present a political problem for Buttigieg. Former San Antonio Mayor Julián Castro is also in the race; Castro has Cabinet experience in the Obama administration, where he served as Secretary of Housing and Urban Development.

Mayor Buttigieg has a lot to offer to voters in terms of having a refreshingly clear viewpoint and being an outstanding public speaker. His visceral authenticity to audiences as a public speaker is a political asset that few others in the race can match, or have matched yet. For all of his departures from the norm, twenty-two other past U.S. presidents have had military experience, the second largest group by occupation after lawyers.[6]

Mayor Pete Buttigieg brings experience to the race, and he brings wisdom, but he doesn't bring age. It remains to be seen if that becomes a barrier to primary voters or a boon. If he doesn't win the primary, there are solid political reasons that he could still land a spot on the bottom of the ticket, and he could always mount a potential future run for statewide office in Indiana or seek a White House or cabinet position in a future Democratic administration.

DEFINING MOMENTS IN PETE BUTTIGIEG'S POLITICAL CAREER

The South by Southwest festival happens annually in Austin, Texas, with a film festival, the world's largest music festival, and interactive media exhibits. It's not typically associated with presidential politics. But that changed when CNN decided to host a trio of nationally televised, prime time presidential candidate town hall events there on March 10, 2019, at the Moody Theater.

Nobody expected much to happen from the trio of candidates that included Rep. Tulsi Gabbard (D-HI) and former Rep. John Delaney (D-MD), both of whom registered at or under 1 percent support in the *Des Moines Register* and CNN poll of likely Iowa caucus goers released the day before the town hall.[1] That poll also showed only 1 percent support for the third of the trio, Pete Buttigieg and his exploratory campaign.

It wouldn't be Buttigieg's first national television appearance. On ABC's top-rated daytime show *The View*, host Joy Behar cheerily called him, "The first gay candidate, that we know of, that we know of . . ." while the surprised Indiana mayor's eyes went wide.[2] But that appearance, just a week after launching his campaign and forty-one days before the South by Southwest town hall, didn't generate a massive national buzz, nor did the others he did in the previous seven weeks. None had succeeded in boosting Buttigieg significantly in the polls.

Little did they know that Mayor Pete's performance on CNN that night would be special, and it would vault him onto the primary debate stage only six days later. Buttigieg's poll numbers in Iowa since then have averaged in the low teens, putting him in the top five candidates out of a twenty-one person field as of early May 2019.[3]

The day of the town hall, on a Saturday, Buttigieg's campaign posted a video to Facebook urging his thirty-one thousand supporters to donate to his campaign before the CNN town hall the next day because, "I've got a lane all to myself, here, as the only left-handed, gay, millennial, Maltese-American, Episcopalian war veteran considering a run. Why run? Because it's time to focus on the future. Because there's no going back. Our country needs a fresh start. Are you ready to walk away from the politics of the past?"[4] The mayor spoke to the camera in a fast-moving thirty second pitch, with bold white letters on the screen flashing out to spell what he said, "It's time for a new generation of American leadership. Now. Join Us."

CNN's Jake Tapper started the town hall by asking what quite possibly every person Mayor Buttigieg meets asks: "How do you pronounce your name?" However, he asked it in a subtle way that contrasted the mayor's pronunciation ("boot-edge-edge") with the the way his husband pronounces it, "buddha-judge." Buttigieg deftly replied in a way that made Tapper compliment him for being "very diplomatic" and noting that he "didn't throw his husband under the bus," drawing knowing laughter from the crowd about the delicacy of spousal relations in political campaigns.

With the ice broken, Tapper introduced the first audience question, which was about the obvious: Is the mayor of a hundred-thousand-person city really prepared to handle the job of being president of the United States? With a blend of seriousness and humor at the sad state of the presidency today, Buttigieg gave an answer that not only satisfied the town hall audience, but turned his perceived inexperience on its head:

> [I] would argue that being a mayor of a city of any size, especially in the strong mayor system we have in my community, where there's no one else to call when there's an emergency or a major policy issue, is arguably the best kind of preparation you can have. I know that it's more traditional to maybe come from Congress, to have a background in Washington, but I would also argue that we would be well served if Washington started to look more like our best-run cities and towns rather than the other way around. [APPLAUSE]
>
> Think about it. One thing you've never heard of is a city shutting down because they couldn't agree on a policy. Right? It's literally unthinkable. We would never do it. [APPLAUSE]
>
> We couldn't do it, because we deliver water, and you need water to live. So we just figure things out. And that's the kind of attitude that I think we need more of in

Washington today. I get that it might sound a little cheeky as the youngest guy in this conversation, but I actually think experience is one of the best reasons for somebody like me to be in this. I have more years of government experience under my belt than the president. [LAUGHTER]

I've also got more years of executive government experience under my belt than the vice president [Pence] and more military experience than anybody to walk into that office on day one since George H.W. Bush. So I get that I'm the young guy in the conversation, but I would say experience is what qualifies me to have a seat at this table.[5]

A later fact-checking report by South Bend's ABC affiliate was inconclusive about Buttigieg's remark about having more military experience than former President George W. Bush, who served in the Texas Air National Guard but never deployed for combat.[6] Unfortunately, not all of the factual questions about the mayor's service have been answered or can be answered through public records requests. But his point remains, and that answer crossed the Rubicon; it was a clear answer to a baseline question about experience that the mayor had probably been fielding only a few times daily for the six weeks since he'd begun his exploratory campaign. Then the town hall began in earnest, with an audience question about his opinion on the impact of automation on manufacturing employment, something that is only expected to grow in the future.

Buttigieg proceeded to meticulously explain why he understands the trauma of job loss as a native son of South Bend. Scientific research shows that losing a job is greater than simply losing an income, and how employment benefits need to become portable, which includes extending Medicare for All to workers to free them from the fear of death if they lose a job and floated the concept of universal basic income. It's a concept that exalted conservative economist Milton Friedman first proposed in the 1960s, and the CNN host followed up with a pointed question about it. The mayor carefully explained that it's a good idea, but "we're at the outset of learning about what these policies could do on the ground."

After a follow up question from the audience about Medicare for All, and one about his recently deceased father from Malta, "this tiny nation, the place Buttigieg is a common name," the queries turned to Mayor Pete's "lane all to himself" as the first out major party presidential candidate. An economics professor asked him how his primary candidacy—which, if successful, would make him the first gay nominee—would affect all lesbian, gay, bisexual, transgender, and queer (LGBTQ) people in an era when the Republican Party is perceived by some as punishing people for their sexuality and gender identity. He replied:

> [T]hat intimate thing in our lives exists by the grace of a single vote on the U.S. Supreme Court. And it's a reminder that the freedoms—you know, our conservative friends talk about freedom a lot, but they're always talking about "freedom from," as if government is the only thing that can make you unfree. That really important freedom

in my life, the freedom to marry, came about because of choices that were made by policymakers who had power over me and millions of others.

Now, we got to marriage equality. I would not have guessed that that would be possible. Frankly, when I first got into politics, elected politics at the beginning of this decade, in Indiana, in—in Mike Pence's Indiana, I thought you could either be out or you could be in office, but you couldn't be both. I came out in the middle of a re-election campaign, because it was just that time in my life when I had to do that. Pence was governor. We weren't sure what it would do to my political future in a socially conservative community.

I wound up getting re-elected with 80 percent of the vote.

Tapper brought in another audience member with a follow-up question about LGBTQ issues. History will record Pete Buttigieg's response as the viral moment that transformed his campaign from a million to one long shot in to a candidate that nobody can ignore in the early stages of the 2020 Democratic primary.

"Thank you for your service and your position in politics," Dr. James Doty stated as prelude. "The question I'd like to ask you is, as you pointed out, Vice President Pence is obviously quite conservative. . . . In regard to these conservative views, in regard to religion and in sexuality, in comparison to the average voter or the voter in Indiana, let's say: Are his views an aberration? Or is this really representative of the state?" asked the Stanford University neurosurgeon, intoning a question that many people outside Indiana are curious about in the wake of its former governor having signed a law validating antigay discrimination in 2015. "Or are most people more like you in your more liberal views about us as humans?"

"Please don't judge my state by our former governor," replied Buttigieg to a mixture of laughter that led to applause, sixteen minutes into the one-hour town hall. He explained his role in the fight against social extremism after Gov. Pence passed that 2015 law. Then, Jake Tapper asked a follow-up: Who would be a better president, Pence or Donald Trump? "Ugh," replied the mayor, scratching his chin, eyes bulging at being put on the spot by the CNN host's question. "Does it have to be between those two?" replied Buttigieg. "Politics is about choices, man," snapped Tapper. The mayor's answer went viral:

I mean, I don't know. It's really strange. Because I used to at least believe that he believed in our—I've disagreed with him ferociously on these things, but I thought, well, at least he believes in our institutions and he's not personally corrupt. But then—but then how could he get on board with this presidency? How could somebody who— you know, his interpretation of scripture is pretty different from mine to begin with. OK, my understanding of scripture is that it is about protecting the stranger and the prisoner and the poor person and that idea of welcome.

That's what I get in the gospel when I'm in church. And his has a lot more to do with sexuality and, I don't know, a certain view of rectitude. But even if you buy into that, how could he allow himself to become the cheerleader of the porn star presidency?

[Is it] that he stopped believing in scripture when he started believing in Donald Trump? I don't know. I don't know.

Pete Buttigieg judged Pence according to his own moral code. He adjudicated the vice president to be a hypocrite. The mayor's answer to Tapper's question combined some real soul searching and a viral tagline that reminds the audience that the Republican in the Oval Office has committed unseemly crimes to cover up his even more unsavory personal life. It wasn't a scripted remark and it's not in his book. It was just Mayor Pete being himself, thinking on his feet, consulting his faith, and unafraid of the future consequences of wagging tongues. In short, it was a very midwestern answer, but delivered with a spicy zinger.

The CNN town hall went to break, and continued on for another thirty minutes after that answer, but the moment still lives on. In just the fifty days afterward, a Google News search shows that 2,240 stories reference the term "porn star presidency." Vice President Pence quickly responded, amplifying the impact of Buttigieg's one-liner and raising his national profile even further.

Eventually, the Reverend Franklin Graham, Jr., who is a prominent evangelical Christian leader and anti-LGBTQ crusader, got into the act, making negative comments about the mayor, which further endeared him to the Democratic Party's base voters.

Tapper's audience continued to pepper Buttigieg with questions that night: about his work for global management consulting firm McKinsey & Company; about Venezuela (he condemned National Security Advisor John Bolton's involvement, which he said was "highly disturbing"); about his ideas for expanding and depoliticizing the Supreme Court; about his service in Afghanistan (he said that he "crossed the wire" 116 times, which is military slang for leaving the base in a war zone) and about the state of peace talks there; about the burden on veterans in general, and a lot more.

Mayor Buttigieg finished the town hall, which was the last of the group of three that night, and left the stage to shake hands and mingle with the crowd.[7] "@PeteButtigieg doing himself a world of good with this @CNN Town Hall," wrote two-time Democratic National Convention CEO Leah D. Daughtry on Twitter as the broadcast drew to a close that night.[8]

What made Pete Buttigieg's town hall different from his two peers? Besides the whopping $600,000 that Mayor Pete raised in the following twenty-four hours? When he joined CNN's Jake Tapper on stage, expectations were low and the broadcast began by hitting him with every question that would occur to voters after hearing that the young mayor of a small city is running for president. Not only did he answer them, but he deftly explained why those issues are some of his potential strengths. And when it comes to explanations, the mayor showed that he could deliver them without putting people to sleep or making his pre-written material sound like, well, pre-written material. In fact, some of his most comprehensive responses to those questions were his almost verbatim positions from his book, *Shortest Way Home*.

South Bend's mayor demonstrated clearly that he's qualified to be named in the debate about who should become America's next commander-in-chief with his combination of down-home demeanor and keen intellect. Google searches for the not-so-easy-to-spell Buttigieg jumped remarkably the following day, eclipsing those for the top three Democratic candidates at the time, former Vice President Joe Biden, Senator Kamala Harris, and Senator Bernie Sanders.[9] Ironically, Tapper had asked Buttigieg at the town hall about a prizewinning essay that he wrote about Sanders in 2000, calling it when he "first became famous." Mayor Pete's reply? "I'm not sure if I'm famous now, but thank you." He was. The pundits raved about what CNN called his "star turn." Eric Bradner quoted the following reactions in an article for CNN:

> Amanda Litman, a former Clinton aide who co-founded the group Run for Something—which helps first-time candidates—tweeted: "I'm still not sure if Pete Buttegieg (sic) should be president yet but nearly every answer he gives (and his entire book!) is an argument for why young people can & should run for local office. He makes it sound fun, meaningful, and totally doable."
>
> "I have rarely seen a candidate make better use of televised Town Hall than @PeteButtigieg is on @CNN tonight. Crisp, thoughtful and relatable. He'll be a little less of a long shot tomorrow," tweeted David Axelrod, a

former adviser to President Barack Obama and a senior political commentator at CNN.

"Without a doubt, we need to hear more from @PeteButtigieg on a national stage," tweeted Jess O'Connell, a former Democratic National Committee CEO and former executive director of EMILY's List.[10]

"Everyone should be watching @CNN right now. @PeteButtigieg is absolutely killing this town hall," gushed author and UNH English professor Seth Abramson to his more than half-million followers.[11] "I'm not endorsing anyone or putting anyone else down—at all—I'm just saying this guy, who I didn't know anything about before tonight, seems extremely impressive. So many smart ideas."

Ironically, much of the mayor's remarks that night were about defusing the spectacle of politics in Washington and replacing them with his low-key, high-minded brand of pragmatic politics to improve people's lives.

The *Washington Post's* reported opinion writer Jennifer Rubin wrote, "Buttigieg was impressive because he spoke directly, without political buzzwords or hyperbole. He actually answered questions and he had a comfort level with policy, even foreign policy(!), that many other candidates don't." She continued:

> *Maybe that sounds really smart only because we've gotten so used to such half-baked, slogan-driven answers. But then again, campaigns are graded on a curve. If he sounds more informed and sensible than others, well*

> *then he deserves support. He addressed the "Aren't you too young?" question a couple of times, but the real answer should be this: He's a lot smarter than many people in the race and, coming from a red state, has a real understanding and respect for Republicans.*
>
> *Buttigieg is still the longest of long shots. However, he deserves to be taken seriously. If we want a celebrity or someone who's never had an original thought in his life or someone who thinks we can have unicorns and rainbows, well, then shame on us.[12]*

Rubin broke up with the GOP in May 2016 when it became apparent that Donald Trump would be the party's presidential nominee, and her blog used to be called "Right Turn." She's the kind of centrist voters that many Democrats seek to attract, yet he drew some of her highest praise in her column for his "cogent" explanation of Medicare for All, which she called "specific, rational, and personal."

"Pete Buttigieg is the human rebuttal to everything Mike Pence stands for," wrote CNN's Michael D'Antonio. He noted that the contrast between the current VP and the mayor of South Bend go far beyond just religion, lifestyle, party, or mannerisms:

> *Different as they are when it comes to religion, Pence and Buttigieg are more widely separated when it comes to their approach to government and politics. Pence campaigned three times before he won election but once he*

got into his first office, Congress, he did little active governing. Indeed, during 12 years in office he didn't author a single successful bill. His single term as governor of Indiana was noteworthy mainly for the RFRA debacle and his inattention to problems, including a water pollution crisis in East Chicago and an HIV outbreak in the rural southern part of the state.

In contrast to Pence, Buttigieg has been an active, ball-of-fire mayor who built and refurbished more than 1,000 abandoned homes in 1,000 days and then led the rebirth of a dying downtown. South Bend became a Rust Belt success story. An old Studebaker plant is a center for high-tech start-ups and Buttigieg is trying to bring the train line that connects South Bend airport to Chicago into the city center.[13]

In direct contrast to his opponents that night on the debate stage, Buttigieg was the only one of the three who made a campaign donation pitch on the stage.[14] In fact, it happened during the last town hall question that March evening in Texas when Allie Runas, a senior at University of Texas in Austin, asked him an open ended question. "What do you wish you knew before going into politics and running your first race?" Mayor Pete's answer was revealing:

Wow. Well, I wish I knew just how challenging the dimension of money in politics can be. It's not just a public policy concern. It's something that affects the way that people in politics have to spend their time.

And by the way, I wouldn't be doing my job well if I didn't mention that since we're not taking corporate PAC money, people who like what they hear tonight should go to PeteforAmerica.com and [donate].

(APPLAUSE)

Because in order to get invited to the debate stage, we've got to show that we've had at least 65,000 people donating at any level, which I actually think is great, because it's not just about how many zillions you can raise, but how many people you can get to believe in the idea you should be there.

Obviously, it worked out well.

As of May 5, 2019, there are seventeen out of the declared twenty-two candidates qualified for the first of twelve Democratic 2020 primary debates. That group of twenty-two counts those who are either declared, have an exploratory committee—which is functionally the same as running—or have shown serious intention of entering the race.

The CNN town hall was on a Sunday night, and by the following Saturday, Buttigieg became an early qualifier for the debate by collecting sixty-five thousand donations from at least two hundred donors from each of at least 20 different states. A candidate can also qualify by polling 1 percent in three different DNC-approved surveys, though there are stricter criteria as the debate fills up to screen out the bottom finishers, among which Mayor Pete's campaign will never sit. He's one of nine qualifiers with both the polling and donations met, and there are eight who only make the polling minimum.[15]

There is an element of Pete Buttigieg's success after his consequential CNN town hall appearance that has been reported, but not widely disseminated: he planned for how to take advantage of this particular CNN appearance producing a viral moment. The mayor's campaign staff then, of twenty persons, was smaller than that of many of his primary opponents, some of whom have double that number of staffers *just* in the early caucus state of Iowa. So, how did they leverage the national town hall event into a fund-raising windfall with such a small staff and only two offices, one in South Bend and another (smaller) office in Chicago? *The Hill* reports that it was planned:

> *[A] source close to the Buttigieg campaign pointed to the 130 watch parties across 37 states that took place Sunday evening to highlight the mayor's support and how it could grow. The watch parties were all organized by the Buttigieg campaign and its supporters.*
>
> *Buttigieg's grass-roots fundraising team, comprised of more than 5,000 supporters, also used the town hall to train up on how to fundraise, the source close to the campaign said, adding that the campaign will continue to use a strategy of digital and grass-roots organizing built from the ground up.*
>
> *"I have real questions about if someone can jump*

*from a smallish but iconic city mayor to [president], but
he has earned a spot in the conversation and will be on
the VP shortlist if he doesn't emerge as the nominee,"
the source added.*[16]

Therefore, it is fair to conclude that the mayor's overnight success after his CNN town hall appearance wasn't just the result of his work on the stage, but also in his fledgling campaign's solid planning for what would happen off the stage, on the internet, across the country. That is one of the central themes of his candidacy, and he proved it: that even the mayor of a small city in northern Indiana is qualified to be a presidential nominee because he can take what worked on the local level and scale it up across America.

Right after Mayor Pete made his short fund-raising pitch, he gave his concluding remarks to the open-ended question about what he wished that he knew entering politics, which turned out to be his closing remarks for the entire debate. In just a few words, they showcase the hallmark of Buttigieg's speaking skills: concise words with keen insight delivered in a manner that any voter can relate to:

*[T]he thing I've learned through the process—and I wish
I could say to myself when I was in my 20s trying to figure out if somebody like me had a place in public life—is
that it turns out that everybody, including the most
impressive people that you will encounter, deal with,
negotiate with, or even compete with in public life, they're*

just people. We're all just people. And that's what politics is really about.

It's why I'm trying to take the way we talk about our politics off of the kind of the Washington show and back to the level of everyday life, because that's why the political process matters. And the more we can keep our focus on that, the better I think our country will be for it.

Mayor Pete Buttigieg broke out of the pack with his CNN town hall efforts. Since then his polling numbers have eclipsed a luminary pack of senators, U.S. representatives, and governors. Though he had been in numerous national news stories before that night, none of them resulted in his presently elevated reputation as a top contender for a spot on the Democratic ticket in 2020. The Buttigieg campaign's carefully prepared efforts to turn the candidate's political strengths into quantifiable numbers like donations, new social media followers, and an early ticket to the Democratic 2020 debate stage marked the culmination of a two-year effort by the mayor to transform himself from a quirky regional politician of note into a serious national politician.

POLICY: CAMPAIGN PLATFORMS

Mayor Buttigieg unveiled a detailed policy platform in May 2019, four months after launching his presidential exploratory committee. All twenty-seven issues that he opines upon are framed around three main "pillars" which he announced in January when embarking on his campaign: freedom, security, and democracy.[1] It's a platform that is evocative of President Franklin Delano Roosevelt's famous "Four Freedoms" speech in 1940.[2] Each issue is presented as defining its meaning through the lens of those three pillars, meant to emphasize upon the reader how politics translates to the real world for voters.

Pete Buttigieg's freedom agenda includes his positions on health care, the ability to seek higher education, the freedom for consumers to be protected, racial justice, and civil rights. The mayor presents security issues as those pertaining to matters ranging from housing to elections to gun laws and criminal justice reform. Buttigieg's democracy agenda includes overturning *Citizen's United*, ending gerrymandering and the electoral college, and a host of systemic political changes.[3]

As is fitting for a government executive, Mayor Pete's policy platform is more of an agenda than a specific set of plans. This is in contrast with his competitors, who are current or former senators, and the front-runner, who has not released any policies as of mid-May 2019. Some of his ideas are to support existing legislative proposals, others are studies. In certain areas, Buttigieg would simply enforce existing laws, while other ideas of his would require new legislation to implement.

FREEDOM

Pete Buttigieg highlights ten issues related to freedom, many of which are akin to the kinds of issues that FDR discussed when he called for "freedom from fear." They include issues like investing in teachers, reproductive rights for women, and gender equality. It also touches on infrastructure and labor rights, which have dwindled precipitously throughout the Midwest.

On the issue of health care, his top issue in the freedom section, Mayor Buttigieg supports a move toward a single-payer health-care system, which he calls "Medicare for All Who Want It." He described his plan to a CNN town hall audience in Austin, Texas, as the "best way" to move toward a Medicare-for-all system is to, "take some flavor of Medicare, you make it available on the exchange as a kind of public option, and you invite people to buy into it."[4]

Ten other presidential candidates also support some sort of version of single-payer and all of the Democratic nominees support one form of universal health coverage or another; only former Vice President Biden hasn't taken a position on it by mid-May 2019.[5]

"Freedom," writes the mayor's website, "means the ability to organize in order to hold employers accountable and advocate for fair pay." He supports Congress passing a modern version of the National Labor Relations Act, which guaranteed the right of Americans to organize, and if they must, to strike. Every Democrat running is supportive of the labor movement in general, though Buttigieg has a clear pro-worker stance in his campaign. "Workers here are interested in the same things any American is interested in," Buttigieg told the Kansas Democratic Party Washington Days event as its keynote speaker in March 2018. "You see a lot of signs of, I think, energy in the movement. But the Democratic Party and organized labor need to make sure they are in dialogue and working together."

Thus far, the only union endorsement in the race has gone to Biden, when the International Association of Fire Fighters weighed in on his side right after he declared his candidacy in late April 2019. No doubt, the mayor is aiming to gain the endorsements of some of America's largest remaining unions, those of public school teachers, with his backing for "federal support for higher teacher pay, targeted to districts where it will bring the most benefit."

As for infrastructure, Buttigieg wants to ensure access to drinking water and safe roads, planning to make a "major federal investment in clean water and wastewater infrastructure, transportation and mobility, rural broadband, and climate adaptation and resilience."

Mayor Pete has a robust women's rights platform. It includes the freedom for women to make their own choices about reproduction without government interference, and support for repealing the "Hyde Amendment," which is a Republican law that keeps abortion providers from receiving federal funding, except in cases of rape, incest, or to save the mother's life.[6] The Obama-era Lilly Ledbetter Act extended the time that women have to file gender pay discrimination lawsuits.[7] Buttigieg would take that idea one step further to promote gender pay equity is to encourage passage of a law forcing companies to release disclosures of gender-based pay disparities. That would greatly assist women attain equal pay by making it easier to enforce Title VII of the Civil Rights Act of 1964 by giving women the information they need to go to court if they're being paid unfairly.

The mayor also wants to advance freedom through his racial-justice platform, which would create a commission to propose reparations policies for African Americans and close the racial wealth gap. He listed seven different issues he wants to address:

- Invest in entrepreneurship and home ownership
- Eliminate health disparities, including in maternal and infant health
- Defend affirmative action and combat the opportunity gap
- Protect and expand voting rights
- Support self-determination of indigenous populations
- Redress inequality in our criminal justice system
- Dismantle the prison-industrial complex to end the crisis of mass incarceration

With consumers' rights and freedom in mind, Buttigieg proposes to get Congress to overhaul the notoriously pro-business Federal Arbitration Act. The rest of his consumer protection proposals would merely require appointing a new head of the Consumer Financial Protection Bureau, which his primary opponent Senator Elizabeth Warren (D-MA) created from the ground up.

Lastly, Mayor Buttigieg has a well-crafted plan to restore freedom to love and freedom to be who you are. Under the Trump Administration, LGBTQ rights have been sharply curtailed; Buttigieg would get rid of the ban on transgender persons in the military, encourage the Equality Act to become a law, and step up enforcement of antidiscrimination laws already on the books, including existing provisions in the Affordable Care Act.

"When I was in the military, the people I served with could not have cared less whether I was going home to a girlfriend or boyfriend," he continued telling the *Washington Blade*.[8] "They just wanted to know that I was going to be someone they could trust with their lives and vice-versa."

"My experience is if you can do your job you can do your job," said Buttigieg to South Bend's ABC affiliate station in June 2017 after President Trump abruptly tweeted the new, discriminatory military policy.[9] "In the military one reason why it's been a force for different kinds of Americans coming together is you have Americans working side by side to get something done and that's all that matters."

SECURITY

Fighting climate change is a top priority for Mayor Buttigieg's platform on security. He takes a great angle by stressing how important it is to fight climate change due to the fact it's a national security issue, combining it with his personal experience as a mayor fighting flooding. "Speaking to you as a mayor who found myself compelled to open the emergency operations center of my city twice in two years," he bluntly explained to Public Radio International during the campaign,[10] "for floods that we were told were 500-year to 1,000-year floods—happening back-to-back—don't tell me climate is not a security issue."

Buttigieg has often framed the Green New Deal as an opportunity for new jobs in labor unions. "What the Green New Deal gets right, is it recognizes that there's also an economic opportunity," he told Fox News in a March 2019 interview about Rep. Alexandria Ocasio-Cortez's (D-NY) plan for America to confront climate change head-on.[11] "Retrofitting buildings means a huge amount of jobs for the building trades in this country." It's the kind of messaging that national Democrats need to sell to voters if they want to make the Green New Deal plan a reality. Uniquely in the field, Buttigieg approaches climate as a "long term" problem that will especially impact younger Americans for the years to come, noting that he won't be the current president's age until 2054.

The mayor lists foreign policy as a major security issue, which he wants to reorient to put the "values, goals, and national security interests of American citizens above personal political interests." Even so, he only lists a single vague paragraph of ideas about reinventing institutions, and doesn't address America's relations with any specific country, ally or adversary. He (and many other candidates) faced media criticism for launching his campaign initially without any policy agenda, and his nonextant foreign policy portfolio is sure to draw attention during the early primary debates. The mayor has acquitted himself decently on-stage when answering questions about foreign policy during town-hall debates, but when a major Israeli-Palestinian clash happened in May 2019, he declined to comment, alongside all but four of his then-twenty-one competitors.[12]

It's the opposite situation for Mayor Buttigieg's plans to frame a secure border policy that is both "compassionate and effective." He wants to see "Dreamers"—kids who've grown up in America with undocumented parents—to be protected as part of comprehensive immigration reform which he says requires Congress to:

- Modernize our immigration laws to reflect today's humanitarian and economic needs
- Restore our global leadership in humanitarian relief for refugees
- End the family separation crisis and evaluate ICE and CBP practices to ensure similar humanitarian crises never happen again
- Reinstate enforcement priorities and prevent arbitrary targeting of immigrant communities by enforcement officials

"Tearing apart a community, a business, and a family will make America worse off, every time," he wrote in a March 2017 op-ed column in *HuffPo*. Buttigieg argued in support of President Obama's use of prosecutorial discretion to help 800,000 children born to undocumented immigrant saying, "Americans of good will, regardless of party, are demanding a better way."[13]

Mayor Buttigieg is a member of Mayors Against Illegal Guns, a group that advocates for gun-control legislation.[14] As a member of the first generation that grew up in fear of mass shootings, he supports extremely strict background checks, intense psychological testing, and extensive training for those who want to own guns in America. Planned security improve-ments would also include a renewed assault weapons ban and a nationwide gun licensing system. Buttigieg also supports a new federal "red flags" law that allows for courts to rule that high-risk people may not possess a fire-arm, a reform that even Florida passed in 2018.

Having a military background like Lieutenant Buttigieg has could be extremely helpful when it comes to combating the gun violence epidemic in America. He also has a keen sense of what needs to be done to secure the home front for returning veterans, which includes the need to overhaul the VA health system.

On the election security front, the mayor's platform is a short, but an effective concept: a paper trail on every ballot. He also proposes discourag-ing foreign election interference with sharp consequences to any country who might see 2016 as a model.

Mayor Pete's campaign site weighs in on major economic security issues, supporting a $15 minimum wage and promoting "ensuring every American family has safe, affordable housing." His housing idea is to ask Congress to enact new tenant protections, as well as to fund a national investment into affordable housing construction.

Criminal justice reform is the mayor's most detailed policy proposal because security requires a "fair and racially equitable justice system." Buttigieg's goal in that arena would be to "create incentives for states to reverse mass incarceration and abolish policies perpetuating racial inequal-ity and disparities in the criminal legal system." He lists twelve different remedies on his issues website:

- End mandatory minimum sentences for certain offenses
- Legalize marijuana and address the harmful effects of its criminalization
- Reform pretrial detention, including cash bail
- Significantly increase federal support for community-based reentry programs
- Abolish the death penalty
- Prevent discriminatory police practices
- Increase police accountability for misconduct
- Reduce use of solitary confinement, including abolishing its prolonged use
- End overreliance on parole, probation, and supervised release
- Eliminate the private prison industry
- Ban the box
- Reduce fines, fees, and other ways that states criminalize poverty

In particular, Mayor Buttigieg has been a fierce opponent of the death penalty. "It is time to face the simple fact that capital punishment as seen in America has always been a discriminatory practice," he said in a speech to the National Action Network, a civil rights group founded by the Reverend Al Sharpton, an MSNBC weekend host.[15] "We would be a fairer and safer country when we join the ranks of modern nations who have abolished the death penalty." Still, the death penalty more of a state justice issue than a federal one, since there have only been three federal executions since 1963; all of them happened in the federal prison in the western Indiana city of Terre Haute between 2001 and 2003.[16]

Most of the Democratic candidates running for office want to legalize marijuana in America. "The safe, regulated, and legal sale of marijuana is an idea whose time has come for the United States," the *Boston Globe* quoted the mayor as saying, "as evidenced by voters demanding legalization in states across the country."[17]

Lastly, Mayor Buttigieg believes that "security means keeping communities safe from all forms of violent extremism." His top priority is reversing the Trump administration's rollback of programs to counter domestic terrorism. "All Americans should be able to live without fear of intimidation and violence," his platform reads. "Today, white supremacist extremism and domestic terrorist attacks are on the rise, threatening both our citizens and the very soul of the nation. We need to heal the divides between our communities and work with religious leaders, tech companies, and other influencers to reduce hate and extremism in our homeland."

DEMOCRACY

The final pillar of Pete Buttigieg's campaign is a slew of democracy reforms aimed at restoring the primacy of the ballot box in American politics. He notes, "the federal government has a responsibility to prevent voter suppression and expand voting rights to give us all a voice in our democracy," which has been its traditional role.

The mayor lists nine reforms, many of which are included in the pending House of Representatives bill H.R.1, the For the People Act. They include reforming many of the Republican Party's worst practices:

- Introduce automatic voter registration
- Expand early voting
- Restore voting rights for the formerly incarcerated
- Institute voting by mail
- Make Election Day a holiday
- Protect birthright citizenship
- Provide access for people with disabilities
- Protect voting rights on tribal lands
- Ensure an accurate and depoliticized Census count

On the front of fighting money in politics, Mayor Buttigieg believes that we need to overturn the recent Supreme Court decision known as *Citizens United*—which ignited a flood of dark money and foreign intervention into our federal elections—and even the 1970s case *Buckley v. Valeo,* which stripped federal election law of its strongest limits on spending. He's also in favor of enacting a small donor match system for federal elections. Buttigieg also supports the mandatory creation of anti-gerrymandering protections in the form of independent redistricting commissions in each state. Gerrymandering happens when politicians choose their voters, most often today for the purpose of discriminating on the basis of race or partisan affiliation.

Another major reform to American democracy on Mayor Pete's agenda would be to give statehood to both Washington, DC—whose license plates bluntly state "Taxation without representation"—and the island of Puerto Rico, a territory has suffered in the wake of its worst disaster in a generation without real congressional representation. He would also abolish the electoral college—the small-state weighted, indirect system of electing presidents—forever.

Buttigieg also proposes to expand national service opportunities for Americans in a manner similar to the Peace Corps, the military, or AmeriCorps until it becomes universal for our nation's youth.

Finally, Mayor Buttigieg backs an unorthodox overhaul to the Supreme Court—which could be enacted by legislation—that would expand the court to fifteen members. Ten Justices would be political appointees in the traditional manner of the nine we have today. The other five new Justices would be selected from the lower courts by those ten appointees.

CONCLUSION

Pete Buttigieg began his first South Bend mayoral campaign without an agenda, and when his candidacy caught fire he rolled out a bullet-point plan, then won the race. The mayor has essentially done the same thing with his presidential primary run, which, perhaps not coincidentally, is being run by the same top adviser, Mike Schmul.

Predictably, the mayor's policy bent is heavily skewed toward the kinds of domestic issues that he knows well from his seven years in office. Notably, he doesn't have much published in the foreign policy realm. It's a topic that will be explored in depth, and at one point as the sole subject of one or more of the dozen planned Democratic primary debates. That means foreign policy could become a political minefield for him, especially if he's making up answers on the fly, an area which is usually one of his strengths. President Bill Clinton faced the same issues during his campaign, as the governor of Arkansas with little experience in foreign policy.

Most of his policies put him squarely within the liberal wing of the Democratic Party as opposed to more moderate candidates like Senator Amy Klobuchar, who doesn't support Medicare for All. Unlike his senatorial opponents, his ideology on national affairs isn't well defined, which could work in his favor over the course of a long election race. Some of Buttigieg's ideas are common sense, the center of his party's thinking, while others are innovative—like his court plan—or combine good politics with pragmatic necessity, like his approach to the Green New Deal and trade unions. Other policy ideas of his, like the "Medicare for all who want it," otherwise known as the "public option," are compromise positions between the liberal and moderate wings of party thought.

Overall, Mayor Buttigieg brings a keen intellect to the issues he's ready to tackle, and voters will have to decide if that's enough for him to handle the issues he hasn't taken a stand on yet.

BACKGROUND AND EDUCATION

Peter Paul Montgomery Buttigieg's path to politics began in South Bend, Indiana on January 19, 1982, when he was born to a pair of University of Notre Dame professors. His father, Joseph A. Buttigieg, emigrated to the United States from the Mediterranean island nation of Malta in the mid-1970s to complete his doctoral studies. His mother, Jennifer Anne Montgomery, met Joseph in 1976 when he moved to New Mexico State University in Las Cruces, where she was a member of the faculty.[1] They married four years later in El Paso, Texas, and soon thereafter moved to South Bend, Indiana, where the couple joined the Notre Dame faculty. They had one child.

Joseph Anthony Buttigieg II was an English professor who authored a book about James Joyce's aesthetics titled *A Portrait of the Artist in Different Perspective*, and who worked diligently on a multi-volume edition of the Italian Marxist theorist Antonio Gramsci's *Prison Notebooks,* a project funded through a major grant from the National Endowment for the Humanities.[2]

As an English professor at Notre Dame, J. Anne Montgomery specialized in linguistics. Montgomery's parents were an Army colonel and a piano teacher. Her son Pete speaks eight languages, plays the piano, and is a war veteran.

Pete Buttigieg is married to a twenty-nine-year-old schoolteacher originally from Traverse City, Michigan, named Chasten Buttigieg née Glezman, whom he wed on June 16, 2018, at South Bend's Episcopal Cathedral of St. James; the *New York Times* covered their wedding as a political event.[3] Mayor Pete came out in a letter to the *South Bend Tribune* in 2015. Just a few months later, he met his spouse on the dating app Hinge, and Chasten—then a grad student in Chicago—and he bonded over Scotch eggs and a minor league ballgame. They live together in a fixer-upper home along with their "skittish rescue mutt" named Truman. Since Buttigieg declared his presidential run, Chasten has grown to become something of an internet celebrity himself, with over 322,000 followers on Twitter.

Pete Buttigieg recounted his upbringing in northern Indiana in his memoir *Shortest Way Home.* As a student, he explored all of the different political parties, and dared to dream in his senior year of high school that a kid from South Bend could make it into the Ivy League. After all, he was both valedictorian and student body class president at St. Joseph High School.[4] It worked. He was accepted to Harvard University on academic merit. But before he could even register for his first class at Harvard, something shocking happened.

Young Pete was invited to the school for a special reception to accept the grand prize in the Profile in Courage essay contest. It was his first brush with fame. He won the prize for writing about the courage a certain Vermont U.S. Representative demonstrated in being the only independent member of

Congress, and one who proudly called himself a socialist when others thought it was a political death knell: none other than his current opponent, now-Senator Bernie Sanders. That controversial (to this day) branding wasn't the act of courage featured in the essay; Buttigieg actually praised Sanders's role in forging bipartisan solutions in Congress. He wrote:

> While impressive, Sanders' candor does not itself represent political courage. The nation is teeming with outspoken radicals in one form or another. Most are sooner called crazy than courageous. It is the second half of Sanders' political role that puts the first half into perspective: he is a powerful force for conciliation and bi-partisanship on Capitol Hill. In Profiles in Courage, John F. Kennedy wrote that "we should not be too hasty in condemning all compromise as bad morals. For politics and legislation are not matters for inflexible principles or unattainable ideals." It may seem strange that someone so steadfast in his principles has a reputation as a peacemaker between divided forces in Washington, but this is what makes Sanders truly remarkable. He represents President Kennedy's ideal of "compromises of issues, not of principles."
>
> Sanders has used his unique position as the lone Independent Congressman to help Democrats and Republicans force hearings on the internal structure of the International Monetary Fund, which he sees as

excessively powerful and unaccountable. He also suc-
ceeded in quietly persuading reluctant Republicans and
President Clinton to ban the import of products made by
under-age workers. Sanders drew some criticism from the
far left when he chose to grudgingly endorse President
Clinton's bids for election and re-election as President.
Sanders explained that while he disagreed with many of
Clinton's centrist policies, he felt that he was the best
option for America's working class.[5]

At Harvard University, Buttigieg felt the pull of politics quickly and gravitated into its prestigious Kennedy School of Government's Institute of Politics (IOP), where fifteen years ago he became its student president. The IOP was a foundational place for future-Mayor Buttigieg's political aspirations and they would follow his career with regular checkups. "One memory I have is watching the movie 'Thirteen Days' with Ted Sorenson and Robert McNamara in the room and having a chance to hear firsthand about some of the most consequential crisis management decisions ever made," he told the IOP's January 2012 newsletter right after his first election win.[6] "There's no way you wouldn't be inspired, I think, to be involved in public service and want to have an impact. I don't think my trajectory would have been the same if it weren't for the IOP."

Pete Buttigieg is running an early campaign that stresses his biography and experiences as a member of the millennial generation growing up in the late 1990s and early 2000s. Part of that is a period of time he detailed in his memoir as the fulcrum of his young life. "I mean, we belong to the generation that experienced school shootings as the norm, right? I was in—in high school when the Columbine shooting happened. I belong to the generation that provided a lot of the troops for the post-9/11 conflicts, the generation that's going to be on the business end of climate change," he told a CNN's viewers during the March 2019 town hall event that vaulted him into the national spotlight.[7] "We don't have the luxury of treating climate change like somebody else's problem. We're going to pay the bill for the unaffordable tax cuts for billionaires that were passed by the last Congress and signed by this president."

Buttigieg made the most of his time at Harvard, and he bounced around the country getting an education in public service and politics, whether it was a journalism internship in Chicago or working on campaigns in New Mexico, Massachusetts, Arizona, and Indiana.[8] He coauthored the IOP's nationwide report on campus politics and co-founded the Democratic Renaissance Project aimed at activating the youth vote, even while participating in intramural sports and teaching civics locally. Pete wrote his senior thesis about viewing the Vietnam War through the lens of the Puritan ideology.

"This place shaped me, so much so that my parents would kind of wryly ask whether I was attending Harvard College or whether I was attending the IOP," he told the *Harvard Crimson's* "Fifteen Minutes" column in a more recent April 2019 interview.[9] When asked why he skipped taking a major in government—unlike many other members of the IOP—he explained to FM, "I did History and Literature because I cared about literature a lot, and I realized almost anything else I wanted to study, I could study it through the guise of history."

Buttigieg got a job with the Kerry/Edwards campaign in 2004 just after graduating from Harvard, and before he enrolled at the University of Oxford as a Rhodes Scholar in late 2005 to pursue a postgraduate degree in politics, philosophy, and economics (PPE).[10] Oxford created the PPE curriculum in the 1920s to train future leaders. Their prestigious program which has graduated multiple Prime Ministers of the United Kingdom, as well as of Australia, Pakistan, Myanmar and other nations, and one U.S. President, Bill Clinton. Buttigieg's memoir carefully explained the kind of education he received in precise rhetorical polishing at the world's second-oldest university. His opponent, the former mayor of Newark, Senator Cory Booker (D-NJ) is also a Rhodes Scholar.

The mayor told CNN that while he was baptized in the Catholic faith as a child, by the time he got to Oxford, he didn't "view myself as a Catholic."[11] It was there that he began attending services at Christ Church, which was nearby his college, Pembroke. When Buttigieg returned to America after graduation and moved back to South Bend, he eventually joined the Anglican church of St. James around 2009.

Pete Buttigieg famously speaks eight languages, including Spanish, Italian, French, Maltese, Arabic, and Norwegian. He learned Norwegian while studying at Oxford according to a roommate, by reading a book they left on the toilet.[12] The future politician was also a curator of the dormitory's "whiskey library," an avid fan of his father's muse, James Joyce, and even his esteemed colleagues were impressed by his political gifts. The *New Yorker* magazine reported: "Katharine Wilkinson, an author and an environmentalist, remembered a debate Buttigieg participated in, on the subject of 'democratic policy, or the future of the Democratic Party, or something.' She said, 'I thought, Holy shit, I'm out of my depth. This guy's, like, really freaking impressive.'" Oxford conferred upon him a Master of Arts honors degree he finished first in his class.

Buttigieg left college and, rather than going into politics, took a well-paid position with the global management consulting firm McKinsey & Company. While the company has a more controversial reputation today than when he joined, Buttigieg's specialty was anything but; he specialized in grocery pricing, in addition to the kind of varied problem-solving work in which the firm engages.

"What I did learn a lot about was business and the power of business in order to propel prosperity and help grow our economy. And I believe that business, working within the right framework of the rule of law, is the engine of our growth," he explained to voters in Austin, Texas, during the fateful CNN town hall that propelled him to the upper echelon of early primary polling.[13] "So I think that on the ground knowledge of how to get something done that I maybe began to get in the business community, but really put to work in public service at the local level will be useful. . . ."

But he explained in *Shortest Way Home* that commuting from South Bend, where he had moved back home to take advantage of cheap rent while traveling the world as a consultant, didn't hold the allure of public service and public office. In 2008, he volunteered for Barack Obama's successful presidential campaign. The following year, he signed up for the Navy Reserve. There's not a lot of independent information available about Buttigieg's naval service, but in his book, he recounted the story of his family history of military service as a major motivating factor to join as well as telling the impression made by Harvard's many reminders of its past students who served the country's armed services.

It would be one of President Obama's signature successful crisis management decisions that spurred Buttigieg to quit McKinsey and reenter the political realm in 2010 for his first election race, and it would be a statewide run. The president's auto bailout wasn't enduringly popular, but it worked, preserving a million jobs and resulting in a sharp reversal in fortunes for America's big three auto companies in Detroit, which have an outsized presence in Indiana.[14] However, the Indiana state treasurer Richard Mourdock is a Republican who politically took advantage of his position to advocate for a radical plan to disrupt aid Chrysler which would've directly killed four thousand jobs and disrupted nine thousand pensions in Indiana alone.[15] Mourdock spent $2 million on lawyers to fight the Chrysler bankruptcy proceeding, which was nominally aimed at saving the state's pension fund's $6 million in losses in the car company's debt. The lawsuit continued into 2010 to keep serving his political purposes.[16] Pete Buttigieg decided then that he should quit his job and use the year of living expenses he'd saved to run for the position of Indiana state treasurer that year, a job which paid far less than McKinsey.

It would prove to be a race that even Pete Buttigieg couldn't win, during the year that the GOP rallied its base with the Tea Party movement in reaction to President Obama's 2008 victory. Indiana—a state Obama won—was one of its epicenters, and Mourdock rode his expensive lawsuits in the name of saving money, which failed, to become one of its rising stars at the time. Buttigieg slammed Mourdock for using tax money to go on "partisan adventures" and for appearing with the bizarre Glenn Beck, then a Fox news show host. Buttigieg called Mourdock the "last Indiana official who should appear" with the conspiracy theorist, probably because Beck's main business back then was selling gold to panicked buyers.[17] His opponent slammed back, criticizing Buttigieg for not standing up to try and put Chrysler out of business, which no other public official in America tried to do.

So-called "down ballot" races are always a difficult fight for members of the party that is out of power, and even more so in a year without a gubernatorial or presidential race to attract a higher turnout. Buttigieg won over 600,000 votes, but Mourdock defeated him soundly by a margin of 62.5 percent to 37.5 percent, while the Republican Party that year picked up two House seats and an open seat in the U.S. Senate that had been held by Democrats since 2000.[18] Two years later, Richard Mourdock would go on to shock respected thirty-six-year veteran Senator Richard Lugar (R-IN) in the primary, dispatching the Rhodes Scholar who guided America's foreign policy in the aftermath of the Cold War. But Mourdock committed a career-ending mistake with hideous remarks about pregnancy after rape, and lost the general election to Democratic congressman Joe Donnelly.[19] Before Mourdock mortally wounded his electoral prospects in 2012, Pete Buttigieg took advantage of a lucky break and the swell in his name recognition locally to mount a 2011 campaign to become the mayor of South Bend, Indiana.

On December 9, 2010, South Bend's fifteen-year incumbent Mayor Stephen Luecke announced that he would not run for reelection the following year, and Buttigieg (which the local newspaper explained should be pronounced "BOOT-uh-judge") threw his hat into the ring for the May 2011 Democratic primary race almost immediately.[20] South Bend hadn't had a mayoral election without an incumbent since 1987.[21] What he told the *South Bend Tribune* then about his qualifications to be mayor as the youngest candidate in the race, and what he said eerily echoes his early presidential campaign rhetoric:

> Asked how he might do that as mayor, Buttigieg said it's too soon to discuss details of the policies he has in mind. He said he is not worried that voters will be hesitant to support someone so young. "I think my experience is highly relevant to making a difference here," he said. "I think the reason people have asked me to run is because of my private sector experience. There are surprisingly few business people running for office at the local level."

Within a few weeks, the former McKinsey consultant managed to raise over $50,000, over three-and-a-half times what his nearest competitor raised. Pete Buttigieg officially declared his candidacy on January 22, 2011, promising more online services and a focus on strengthening the local economy, but without any specific plans just four months before the primary.[22, 23]

Newsweek published a story that very week declaring South Bend one of America's top 10 dying cities.[24] "South Bend is not dying, and *Newsweek*'s recent report that said we are is based on bad methodology," wrote the young mayoral candidate in a letter to the editor published in the *Tribune*, responding to the factual slight against his hometown.[25] "But this is not an occasion for denial. It's a call to action. We do face problems, big ones, and we need bold leadership to confront our city's challenges."

In late-March 2011, he scored his major endorsement from the city clerk.[26] A week later, the city's chamber of commerce did something it had never done before: endorsed a mayoral candidate, Pete Buttigieg.[27] Professional polling at the start of April 2011 showed him in a virtual dead heat atop the race with 30 percent of expected voters.[28] Three weeks later, Buttigieg reported $229,000 raised toward his campaign, more than all of the other candidates combined, which he told the *Tribune* that he planned to spend on direct mailers with his detailed written plans for the city.[29] His top opponent was the ten-year State Rep. Ryan Dvorak, who only raised $100,000 and campaigned on his superior experience in government over the untested Buttigieg.

Two weeks before the mayoral election, Pete Buttigieg published an op-ed outlining his six-point plan for South Bend in the *Tribune*:

1. We must enable existing employers to grow and create more jobs.
2. We must foster the creation of new businesses in our community.
3. We need mayoral leadership to compete for job-creating investments nationally and globally.
4. We must offer a simple and user-friendly economic development infrastructure.

5. We will confront poverty so that our community provides economic opportunities for all residents.
6. We need to promote and invest in the quality of life that our city offers to residents.[30]

On Easter Sunday 2011, the editorial board of the *South Bend Tribune* weighed in with an endorsement in the Democratic primary for mayor just nine days before ballots were cast, and they picked Pete Buttigieg, writing:

> *[Pete] Buttigieg acquired a truly outstanding education and has both training and experience in economic issues on the national and international levels. As the youngest of the candidates, 29-year-old Buttigieg exudes energy and enthusiasm. But in interviews and forums, it is the depth of understanding and penetrating intelligence of his answers that puts him a bit ahead of the rest of the class. . . .*
>
> *Pete Buttigieg offers more reason to believe the status quo will be discarded and the clearest vision for building a new and better South Bend. Jobs and the local economy are at the top of every candidate's list of challenges. Buttigieg already has fresh, creative ideas to offer on that front, and his diligent style of learning from the voters as he campaigns seems to offer the possibility of more answers from new places and new alliances to serve as catalysts for progress.[31]*

The following Monday after Easter, South Bend celebrated its biggest local holiday: Dyngus Day, an event held at the West Side Democratic & Civic Club and the parallel event Solidarity Day, which celebrates black solidarity. For Democrats, it is the official kickoff of primary campaign season, even though that year the festival fell only eight days before the voting. It's the Polish equivalent of St. Patrick's Day, and locally that means beer (actually a lot of beer) and kielbasa sausages.[32] It also means politics, drawing the likes of 1968 Democratic presidential hopeful Robert F. Kennedy, who used his win in the Indiana primary to become the front-running candidate before being assassinated. Presidents Obama and Clinton also visited South Bend for Dyngus Day. Buttigieg sponsored that year's main Dyngus Day event, advertising his "Pete for South Bend" campaign on all of the West Side club's tickets.[33] The next day, he picked up the endorsement of the South Bend Firefighters Union, Local 362.[34]

By the end of that week, his top opponent went negative against Buttigieg, airing ads criticizing his quarter-million-dollar campaign haul from the city's traditional power brokers, which he shrugged off by saying that his eight hundred donors "span the political spectrum" and that he would "make his own decisions if elected."[35] The following day, Buttigieg landed a major endorsement from former Rep. John Brademas, who used to represent South Bend, whom he named honorary campaign chair.[36]

Indiana has an open primary system, which means that voters of any party and independents may choose which primary in which they vote. When the results arrived, Pete Buttigieg earned a decisive win in a race with double the turnout of previous primary elections. While there was no certain way to tell, estimates said that up to three thousand Republicans voted for him out of out of the 13,957 ballots cast in the Democratic primary, far more than the 655 who voted for the GOP nominee that year. South Bend's Republican primary only attracted 995 total votes; it seems that the Republican candidate, a middle-aged carpenter, had a hard time attracting votes from even his own party. As the *Tribune*'s longtime opinion columnist Jack Colwell wrote, in a column titled "The Factors Behind Buttigieg's Big Win," the Pete for South Bend campaign exceeded expectations:

> With four serious contenders for the Democratic nomination, most projections were that the winner would be the one getting a little over a third of the vote. Buttigieg got 55 percent. Nobody, including Buttigieg, thought as election day dawned that he would win that big. But he had run an almost letter-prefect campaign since entering the race with scant name recognition—and most of those recognizing it not knowing how to pronounce it. Steadily, even if slowly at first, he began to get known and impress those he met, including some big contributors. He raised far more in campaign funding than any of the other contenders.
>
> Buttigieg also built a superior organization for identifying potential supporters and getting them to go to the polls. Key person in those efforts was Mike Schmuhl, Buttigieg's campaign manager and friend going back to the days when they both were students at St. Joseph's High School. Schmuhl had just been campaign manager

for U.S. Rep. Joe Donnelly, D-Granger, in Donnelly's survival of the 2010 Republican tsunami.[37]

Mike Schmuhl was a key contributor to that race, and he would go on to become Pete Buttigieg's key adviser as the mayor's chief of staff for the following two years before leaving to pursue his postgraduate studies. Schmuhl is currently serving as campaign manager of Mayor Buttigieg's presidential run as of May 2019.[38] Jack Colwell concluded his postrace column by explaining how the pile-on of endorsements powered Buttigieg's campaign and his presumed closest opponent's negative campaigning backfired. It was only a primary, but Colwell effectively declared that Buttigieg was going to be the next mayor:

> *Finally, the contest had come down to Buttigieg and state Rep. Ryan Dvorak. Dvorak, without building up to it, turned to negative TV ads and mailings in the closing days. It backfired. Buttigieg responded quickly, lamenting the negative turn and saying that political attacks "don't create jobs, improve schools, reduce crime or fix vacant houses." Buttigieg had the campaign resources to carry that message in TV ads and through the mail. Dvorak slipped to third. And Buttigieg became, well, actually, mayor-elect.*

Six months later, voters went to the polls to pick a new South Bend mayor in the general election where Pete Buttigieg faced Republican opponent

Wayne Curry, a well-liked fifty-year-old carpenter and a Libertarian party opponent. It wasn't close. Buttigieg won over 74 percent of the votes to claim victory just twenty-five minutes after the polls closed.

Not only was the voting nowhere near close, but Buttigieg won every single one of the city's ninety-one voting precincts.[39] While the primary vote had a massive turnout, the general election ballot was only slightly larger, and 25 percent lower than the previous mayoral race. He became the second-youngest mayor in the history of the city that night at the age of twenty-nine, and the youngest head of a city with 100,000 residents in America.

> *"When I entered this race in January, not a lot of people believed that a young man with a funny name who had never held office before could earn the confidence of a community at a turning point,"* he said in his speech at the West Side Club, *"but together we have shown that South Bend can transcend old barriers, move beyond old habits and take a chance on a new way forward."*
>
> *"We know that our survival depends on new thinking, and that's what tonight is about. We're going to lay aside old habits and old divisions, we're going to transcend old rivalries, we're going to abandon old prejudices.*
>
> *"The only way we can recover and surpass what our old prosperity was is with new energy, new options and new alliances. We must take new risks and create new opportunities."*[40]

"It's going to be a great new year for our city, and I cannot wait to roll up my sleeves and get started," wrote Buttigieg in the *Tribune* a week before he was sworn into office.[41] "With a mixture of new faces and experienced public servants, this team will work with departments and citizens to deliver the accountable, transparent, cost-effective, efficient government I envision going forward."

On January 1, 2012, at 5 p.m., Pete Buttigieg was sworn into office at the Century Center, which overlooks the southern bank of the St. Joseph River, to become South Bend's 32nd mayor. He will hold the position until January 1, 2019, when he steps aside for—in all likelihood—his "handpicked" successor James Mueller, who won a plurality of votes in the May 2019 Democratic primary election.[42]

MAYOR OF SOUTH BEND, INDIANA

Mayor Pete Buttigieg took over the top job in South Bend on New Year's Day 2012 during a time of high unemployment, after a year of monstrous blizzards, and right after a mid-major department store chain closed its distribution center in South Bend and put five hundred more people out of work.[1] Unemployment in his northern Indiana hometown never recovered from the "dot-com crash" of the early 2000s, spiked to over 12 percent after the Great Recession, and was sitting near 9 percent when he took office.[2] In the late 1990s, the unemployment rate had dropped under 3 percent. The year he took office, South Bend was shaken by eighteen homicides.[3]

Mayor Buttigieg's first hundred days in office have come in many ways to shape his term of office since then, often in ways that he hadn't imagined at the time. In fact, there's one nagging legal issue that he has been navigating ever since, related to a rookie mistake managing his police chief. His administration has struggled with crime issues, but in a way that is representative of the average results one would expect from other Indiana cities, and not for lack of well-planned trying. The native Hoosier introduced his signature first-term program in his second year in office—South

Bend's Vacant and Abandoned Housing Challenge—and achieved mixed, but generally positive results. While it was ongoing, Lt. Buttigieg spent six months deployed to an active war zone in 2014.

The year 2015 was a reelection year for the mayor, and the conclusion of the mayor's housing initiative wasn't the only major event. In fact, it would become *the* defining year of his term of office. It was a difficult year for racial tensions in America, and the mayor equally had difficulties navigating those fault lines as the supervisor of his city's police department.

But it would be a revelatory year for Pete Buttigieg. He was at the forefront of one of the highest-profile national political fights of the year centered on an Indiana state law signed by Mike Pence, then the state's governor, aimed at legalizing anti-LGBT discrimination. Soon afterward, the mayor published an essay in the local newspaper declaring himself the first "out" major city mayor in Indiana.

In the following two years, Mayor Buttigieg's national profile grew tremendously while his local projects came to fruition. After the startling 2016 presidential election, he ran to chair the national Democratic Party and cemented his rise as a national political figure within the party, along with new political contacts and donors. He still also managed to show South Bend residents concrete results from his increasingly national travels and accountability for how it all came about.

"The 29-year-old former business consultant said his campaign was based on the idea that all types of people throughout the city can pull together to create a better South Bend," wrote the *South Bend Tribune*'s Kevin Allen on New Year's Eve 2011, in the first of what would become over fifteen hundred newspaper articles mentioning Buttigieg over the next seven years.[4] "Buttigieg said it falls on him now to harness that energy and turn it into results. 'I can lead it,' he said, 'but I can't do it without everybody else.'" Bill Moor celebrated in the *Tribune* that he learned how to write the mayor's name without spell-checking (a tongue in cheek but factual statement) and that he hoped Buttigieg would not lose sight of the fact that he's a public servant, not a politician.[5]

THE FIRST HUNDRED DAYS

Mayor Buttigieg faced some of the issues and challenges that would come to define his term of office just days and months into his new term. Only two days after being sworn in, the city's council debated spending millions to rehabilitate South Bend's largest building, the twenty-five-story Chase Tower, as it was then known; it would be the beginning of an ongoing revitalization project that would become a signature success in Buttigieg's term. Later that week, the new mayor proposed significant staff raises to attract and retain talent, a political risk during an era when cities were busy cutting budgets, not spending.[6, 7] That's also when he named Mike Schmul—his then-mayoral and now presidential campaign manager—as his chief of staff.

In his busy first one hundred days on the job, the mayor would appoint a new fire chief, pass his staff pay plan, and change the tradition of how his office delivered its State of the City address. That's also when he began efforts to tackle South Bend's vacant housing crisis, one of the keystones of his term of office, convening a task force to study the problem and make rapid recommendations. Mayor Buttigieg also replaced his police chief during those first hundred days, a controversial decision amid a criminal probe that rocked the city.

The South Bend common council also passed a "special rights" bill that added gender identity and sexual orientation to its municipal human rights ordinance.[8] "In today's economy and today's competition for talent—if we fail that test, if we remain outside the American mainstream any longer—South Bend could be typecast as a prejudiced and backward-looking community," said Buttigieg during the bill's debate, three years before he came out, "and our economic comeback will be that much harder to bring about."[9]

Only two days after South Bend's new human rights ordinance passed, Mayor Pete donned a hoodie and marched down Washington Street alongside Police Chief Darryl Boykins to the Martin Luther King Jr. Center with three hundred demonstrators demanding justice for Trayvon Martin, a young black teenager who had been unjustly killed by George Zimmerman only a month earlier.[10]

But Buttigieg and Boykins didn't talk.

That's because the mayor had just accepted Chief Boykins's forced resignation due to an ongoing FBI criminal probe into his police department for potential violations of the federal law prohibiting wiretapping.[11] In the process, Buttigieg also irked the city's common council for concealing his knowledge of the ongoing federal investigation, which he learned about two months prior, soon after taking office. It's still an ongoing dispute.

THE SECRET TAPES SAGA

Just one day later, Chief Boykins reconsidered his resignation from the South Bend PD, which he joined in 1984 and had risen to lead. Buttigieg declined. Boykins was rehired, but had to accept a difficult demotion to captain.

"It felt stomach-churning," Buttigieg recalled of the night of the 2012 protest, speaking to the *New York Times* during the campaign.[12] "To know that that same day, we were at what even then I understood was going to be the beginning of an incredibly painful and divisive moment of race relations in my city."

Allegedly, four white officers, including the city's head of homicide investigations, were surreptitiously caught on tape making racist remarks, and the chief found out when another his communications director accidentally recorded the calls.[13] He instructed the officer who made the recordings to continue making them. Amazingly, the incident remains unresolved seven years later amid a flurry of lawsuits, and in his book Mayor Buttigieg called the firing the "first serious mistake" he made in office.[14]

In August 2012, pressure built on Buttigieg to release the tapes from his city's common council. Local Google search interest in Mayor Buttigieg hit a peak for his first term in September 2012 after two milestones in the case. He revealed that the U.S. attorney investigating Boykins cleared him of wrongdoing in a letter. Then, the police officers who were recorded filed a lawsuit against Buttigieg and the city alleging that their rights were violated by being recorded, even though they were public officials performing their duties and should generally not expect privacy while doing so.

Also, Captain Boykins later sued Mayor Buttigieg and his chief of staff, Schmul, alleging racial bias. Boykins won a settlement, as did the communications director who made the recordings and the four officers who were secretly recorded. In total, the city of South Bend has paid over $800,000 to date in three different lawsuits, and an Indiana judge is still considering if he will order the tapes released—which the South Bend Common Council has demanded through a subpoena against Buttigieg—at the time of writing in mid-May 2019.[15] The city's legal fees in the case have exceeded $2 million.[16] The officers who were recorded are still fighting to keep the tapes secret as of mid-May 2019. The mayor won't release the tapes without a court order, because he is rightfully afraid that disclosure could violate federal law.

Boykins's former attorney told CNN in 2019 that just based upon a written summary of the of the recordings, "if we've got the head of our metro homicide unit is dropping racial epithets, how long is it going to be before the Innocence Project comes in and starts looking at all these prior convictions?"[17] To this day, neither that attorney nor Mayor Buttigieg has listened to the secret tapes, which he explained at a late April 2019 CNN town hall with Anderson Cooper, along with what he learned from the "secret tapes" dilemma after a member of the audience questioned him about the incident:

> *One of the things I realized was that while I was absorbed in just making sure that we weren't tripping on any landmines related to laws about what you can and can't record, I was, frankly, a little bit slow to understand just*

PETE BUTTIGIEG ★ 73

how much anguish underlay the community's response to this. Because for people in the community, it wasn't just about whether we were right or wrong to be concerned about the Federal Wiretap Act. It was about whether communities of color could trust that police departments had their best interests at heart.

And the more I learned about that, the more I realized that lifting the veil of mistrust between communities of color and our police department had to be one of my top priorities as mayor. It's why we instituted civil rights training and implicit bias training. It's why we implemented body-worn cameras for all of our officers. It's why we directed officers to make more foot patrols and get to know people in these neighborhoods, especially neighborhoods experiencing a lot of crime, not in an enforcement environment, but in a trust-building environment. And a number of other measures, including stepping up our efforts to recruit more minority recruits onto the department itself, something I'm still not satisfied with what we've been able to do so far, so that there's more of that trust.[18]

Unfortunately, as Anderson Cooper pointed out after the mayor finished speaking, as of 2018, only 5 percent of the police in South Bend's department are African American, even though slightly more than a quarter of the community is black. The two following chiefs that have been hired to lead South Bend's police department since Boykin's firing, then demotion, are both white men.

His handling of the FBI's investigation into the police chief erupted onto the national stage during Mayor Pete's presidential campaign after the conservative *Washington Free Beacon* published a detailed story covering the secret tapes.[19] "This mystery around these tapes has been looming over the community for so many years," South Bend councilwoman Regina Williams-Preston told CNN.[20] "It's like a cloud. Because every time there's some kind of incident, you know, it kind of rips that 'band-aid' off and brings us back to this question: Is there clear evidence of some sort of racism and bias inside our police department?"

Buttigieg later took concrete steps to improve the city of South Bend's diversity in hiring when he signed an Executive Order creating an Office of Diversity, using his powers under the city's strong-mayor form of mayor-council government.[21] The mayor hired a talented diversity recruiter named Christina Brooks away from Notre Dame, to be the city's first officer of diversity and inclusion.[22] Brooks created and implemented a three-year, sixty-three-point plan aimed at bringing in more minority police officers, as well as guiding their career paths. In addition, that move has led to ongoing reforms in the city's purchasing practices to include more women and minorities as vendors to South Bend.

MANAGING SOUTH BEND'S PROBLEMS WITH CRIME

South Bend has a gun violence problem and problems with crime. During the mayor's term the number of homicides annually remained constant until dropping in 2018 to half the number as his first year in office.[23] From 2012 through 2018 the number of property crimes in South Bend dropped sharply, but the number of aggravated assaults jumped accordingly. "During Mayor Pete Buttigieg's time in office, the overall numbers of reported crimes have actually dropped," wrote Christian Sheckler for the *South Bend Tribune* in April 2019, noting that there have been some changes in the FBI's crime-reporting standards over the last decade.[24] "In the three years before Buttigieg took office, South Bend police reported an average of 6,845 crimes in the most serious categories tracked by the FBI, according to annual statistics dating back to 2009. Since 2012, Buttigieg's first year in office, the city has averaged 5,890 reported crimes in those categories."

Evaluating city statistics means that it's important to hold a perspective of the impact that state gun laws beyond local control have on violent crimes. Overall, the state of Indiana's gun homicide rate is 15.2 deaths per hundred thousand according to the Giffords Law Center, which rated the state as having the twentieth most permissive gun laws in America.[25] Amazingly, *Guns and Ammo* magazine also rates Indiana as the twentieth best place to own a gun.[26] Next door, Illinois has five times more gun laws than Indiana and a 22 percent lower statewide homicide rate, according to a CNBC study that showed the correlation between fewer gun laws and more gun homicides.[27] In 2015, South Bend's homicide rate ranked twenty-ninth nationally on the list of cities with populations greater than 100,000 with the highest murder rates at 16.79 per hundred thousand, just one spot behind twenty-eighth-ranked Indianapolis.[28]

The mayor started an initiative called the South Bend Group Violence Intervention, which was designed by the National Network for Safe

Communities (NNSC) by a reputable academic criminal justice center. "Why use the term 'Group' instead of 'Gang'?'" asks the mayor's website for the initiative.[29] "Research finds that most homicides and shootings are committed by members of highly active street groups—these groups are gangs, drug crews, and the like. All gangs are groups, but not all groups are gangs." The *Tribune* noted that the number of shootings only dipped slightly after the NNSC program launched, then gun violence levels returned to historical averages a year later and sharply rose in 2017. Many of South Bend's residents feel unsafe, according to a recent study by the city itself.

1,000 HOUSES IN 1,000 DAYS

In February 2013, Mayor Buttigieg announced his signature initiative to repair or demolish 1,000 houses in 1,000 days. By any reasonable standard, it is safe to say that the initiative was a success. But the details demonstrate that success has been due to the learning experience it provided, which showcases one of the mayor's strengths: dealing with critics in good faith and governing with them to find the best outcome. At the time, South Bend was coping with a 14 percent vacancy rate; nearly one out of every seven houses was vacant. Something had to be done. Vacant homes were depressing property values and providing resources to criminals and vagrants, and their numbers grew after the subprime mortgage crisis led to a rash of foreclosures, increasing the stock of abandoned properties.

However, the 1,000 houses in 1,000 days program also demonstrated one of Buttigieg's weaknesses: understanding in advance the impact of his well-intended ideas on communities of color and of lower income.

Councilwoman Preston-Wilson ran for her office specifically due to her anger at the city, and its mayor, for using his program to knock down multiple houses that her husband owned, but couldn't repair quickly enough. Her primary concern: that the mayor's program would lead to gentrification of the city's African American communities. Forty percent of that community's residents fall below the poverty line, double the national average according to a report by the nonprofit Prosperity Now.[30] In the end though, Buttigieg won over even Preston-Wilson, the most critical African American member of the South Bend Common Council most critical of his policies, by relentlessly refining his efforts.

Buttigieg's program ultimately reduced blighted homes by three quarters. He used a combination of code enforcement, a high-tech neighborhood feedback system, training, along with grant and community outreach programs to move past its contentious beginning to improve quality of life for the city's residents.

The 1,000 houses in 1,000 days campaign began as the kind of data driven city program Mayor Pete promised to bring to South Bend, with a task force cochaired by an expert in community development law at Notre Dame. A few days before the task force issued a detailed seventy-eight-page report, the mayor released his plans. Detailed charts, graphs, and images explained the problems associated with an aging housing stock that is vacant or in disrepair.[31] They didn't recommend the mayor's program, opting for ideas like a penalty tax rate on problem homes or a registry for homes owned by out-of-town investors.

Mayor Buttigieg used data acquired in a shrewd partnership with Code for America (CfA), a national nonprofit that brings together technologists and public servants to solve problems, combined with aggressive city code enforcement, to carry out his plan. CfA's Tamara Manik-Perlman went to South Bend and designed a location-based feedback app called CityVoice.[32] The app consists of a combination of paper signs in front of abandoned houses with call in codes to identify the properties and a call in number where people who see the signs can leave messages about those homes, which is all collated in a publicly available website where anyone can listen to the comments. The program was funded with a block grant from the federal Department of Housing and Urban Development as well as state sources.[33] South Bend also provided a detailed instructional guide to residents at the outset, explaining how to acquire vacant homes and resources to search for public data on those residences.[34]

South Bend has since shut down the original websites that collected data, displayed it and reported back to residents, but the Internet Archive's Wayback Machine preserved all of it, including the program's final report.[35] Ultimately, 60 percent of the 1,122 vacant and abandoned homes that South Bend dealt with in 1,000 days wound up being demolished, 39 percent were repaired, and 1 percent were deconstructed.[36] As time went on, the City of South Bend arranged for a truly impressive cocktail of programs to facilitate home rehabilitation and the mayor moved the program's goalposts to better reflect community pressure.

In the beginning, the program focused on demolitions. It included training code enforcement inspectors as asbestos inspectors to detect the carcinogenic mineral often used as a flame retardant in older homes before its deadly properties were discovered. By the summer, South Bend had a code enforcement "blitz" and held "Code 'Super' Hearings" in August 2013. That meant a team of code enforcement officer had to digitize a literally eight-foot-tall stack of paper violation forms.[37] In October 2013, CfA rolled out CityVoice with 250 signs at the homes that the city was uncertain about repairing or demolishing, and fifty calls rolled right in.[38] But even Manik-Perlman's announcement of app rollout expressly acknowledged that the mayor's program was poorly received in the African-American community which was—rightfully, it turns out—concerned that minority neighborhoods fraught with disinvestment already might be targeted for demolition. The mayor glossed over the discontent among South Bend's minority communities over the plan, and didn't mention that they represent a combined 40 percent of the resident population. In fact, *Buzzfeed*'s Henry Gomez reports in April 2019 that the program directly led to Buttigieg's top critic, Regina Williams-Preston, joining local government because of her concerns about gentrification:

> *She pushed for more resources and fewer fines for those eager but struggling to renovate vacant homes. She demanded a deeper understanding of how big redevelopment plans can wipe out the fragile capital accumulations in communities of color.*
>
> *[T]he story of what happened[,] an ambitious white leader literally plowing ahead before addressing concerns in the community of color — is not the story Buttigieg, 37, tells. You won't read about that part in his book. You*

likely won't hear about it when Buttigieg, who would be the youngest and first openly gay president, preaches "intergenerational justice[.]"

Buttigieg has acknowledged some missteps and, to the appreciation of Williams-Preston and others, made changes to make repairing houses an easier and more affordable option. . . . No one says that Buttigieg was guided by racial or sinister motives. But they also don't buy his simplistic narrative, the story in which he's the hero of a model program that could save cities like South Bend. "Everyone wants to find a villain," Williams-Preston said. "This is just how economic development happens. And I'm just constantly telling the administration: If we do what we've always done, we'll get what we've always gotten. And what we have always gotten in cities all across the country is displacement of poor people and people of color."[39]

All of Williams-Preston's husband's homes were knocked down, and local residents pushed back against the city's agitprop that only out-of-town investors would be impacted by the plan to tear down so many homes. But the mayor supported her "100 houses for 500 families" program and came around to giving more weight to the concerns of activists. Both Williams-Preston and another resident, Stacy Odom, who encountered problems with Buttigieg's 1,000 homes in 1,000 days program, told *Buzzfeed News* that they were happy with the mayor's new focus on housing repair programs. "I think he still has a ways to go," Odom told Gomez. Her month-old Odom Community Developers launched with a crew of five to seven laborers who help homeowners repair their properties and fix code problems. "But I do give Mayor Pete credit for having conversations. I've stopped him on the street many times. And he'll stop and he'll talk: 'Call me, whatever. I'll look into it.'" Later, Odom requested $300,000 from the mayor to run her nonprofit; Buttigieg counteroffered at $650,000.[40]

"Common council member Regina Williams-Preston, who has advocated that more city money go toward improving South Bend's neighborhoods, celebrated the program that she said is a result of the 'community coming together with the city government and really understanding the need, listening, and responding.'" wrote Caleb Bauer in early 2019 for the *Tribune,* describing a public event where she and Buttigieg announced a new home repair assistance program.[41] "'We've really begun to connect with people in the neighborhoods,' Williams-Preston said. "The city government, we're not in our ivory tower anymore. We're on the ground, working with people.' The South Bend Home Repair Pilot, run by the city's department of community investment, will use an anticipated $300,000 in federal block-grant money combined with $600,000 from the city to help homeowners repair major safety issues, including repairs to roofs, electrical systems, heating, ventilation, and air conditioning systems and water heaters. . . . Another program, the South Bend Green Corps, will help both renters and homeowners make basic energy and weatherization improvements, provide home assessments and lead tests, and provide education on reducing power bill costs."

Williams-Preston calls her efforts "healthy pressure" and pointed to the residents of South Bend having a higher reason to needle their mayor about his job performance, because he could well become the President one day. "Some people, they're trying to find the dirt on Pete," she told *Buzzfeed*. "I just try to encourage people. If you look at the whole story—any good story—the hero is an imperfect hero, you know what I'm saying? We don't do everything right. The real story here is the fact that the people organized to make a change."

"I'm not sure we got that completely right," said Mayor Buttigieg to the *Christian Science Monitor* in April 2019.[42] "If there's one thing that I would encourage people to look at in the future, [it] is to really find a fair way to fine tune that enforcement because a lot of it almost inevitably falls to the discretion of the code enforcement personnel."

Near the end of the program, the City and Buttigieg held a celebratory press conference outside a renovated home belonging to the Jara family, who spent a year restoring the property, rescuing it from the demolition list.[43] They met the 1,000 homes goal slightly less than two months before the 1,000-day mark in September 2015. "The problem is never 100 percent solved. What is true is that the problem has been addressed," South Bend's NBC affiliate WNDU reports the mayor as saying. "The best possible outcome is what you see in front of you. A family that has shown and really put their sweat equity into it and is going to look after the property." Two months later, the city reached its 1,122th home.

At the end of the Vacant & Abandoned homes program push, South Bend consolidated everything into one easy-to-follow web page and estimated that it would wholly eradicate its nuisance problem of blighted residences by 2020.[44]

"THE HONORABLE LIEUTENANT" GETS DEPLOYED TO AFGHANISTAN

Pete Buttigieg joined the Navy reserves in 2009, a few years before winning his mayoral election. Thanks to an obscure Indiana law, he was able to appoint an acting mayor in 2014 while deployed to an active war zone. Lieutenant Buttigieg served in the Afghanistan Threat Finance Cell while deployed to Kabul for six months on a mission to disrupt terrorist organizations' finance and support.[45] Much of his service record is redacted from public records requests. City Controller Mark Neal became South Bend's acting mayor in his stead.

The lieutenant told military.com that his time in service was "very formative" because of the, "teamwork, [which leads to] understanding how you build a diverse group of people to do a mission, how to make sure people are flexible, that people are communicating well."[46] Being an active mayor didn't lead to any different treatment, but it did lead a few people to give him a gently teasing nickname, "The Honorable Lieutenant."

"There's a healthy amount of razzing when I got there, but within a few days it wore off. You know I was driving and guarding vehicles a lot," is how Buttigieg described his service in Afghanistan. "When somebody got in my vehicle, I don't think they really much cared what my day job was. They just wanted to know if I was gonna keep them safe." Buttigieg explained in his opinion military service helps build a "sense of perspective and a sense of calm" to help deal with any situation.

The interview concludes with a widely circulated photo of Lt. Buttigieg wearing black sunglasses, standing on top of a mountain outcropping in military fatigues with an olive green, camouflage long-sleeve shirt, holding a fully automatic M4 carbine rifle.[47] The M4 is the military variant of the AR-15 rifle, which has been used in nearly all of the largest civilian mass-shootings in America.

"I carried this over there so I wouldn't need to over here," Buttigieg wrote in a viral tweet in mid-June 2016 about that photo, just a few days after the Pulse Nightclub massacre in Orlando, Fl. by a man under FBI investigation who cited ISIS during the attack without any clear linkage to the group.[48] "2nd amendment is not a pass for terrorists to buy AR-15s."

Afghanistan voted for new leadership in an election held while Lt. Buttigieg was there for a taste of electoral politics. The *South Bend Tribune*'s Erin Blasko reported on his service:

> "One of the things that's been pretty inspiring around here, all the Afghans I met in the last few days had their fingers inked to mark that they voted," he says. For some voters, that exercise in democracy came at a high price. According to reports, insurgents cut off the fingers of 11 voters and killed at least 20 more in election-day attacks. The 32-year-old acknowledges the safety concerns in the country. "We are in a war zone, of course, and there are reminders of that all the time," he says. "But I'm also surrounded by trained professionals in the military, and I've also got excellent training. "Part of my morning routine, of course, is I don't leave the room without a gun," he adds.[49]

Numerous state legislators deploy to war zones as part of America's military reserves, but few if any other mayors. Mayor Buttigieg's naval commission and service overseas serve to bolster his credentials for the presidential nomination he's seeking, alongside only two other veterans, Hawaii Army National Guard Major Rep. Tulsi Gabbard (D-HI) and former Marine Captain Rep. Sean Moulton (D-MA), both of whom served in the Iraq War.

2015 STATE OF THE CITY SPEECH

One of Mayor Buttigieg's first acts in office was to separate the annual executive report on the city from the common council's business meetings. The idea was to refrain from intruding on their business meetings, and also to give more focus to the speech itself as a stand-alone event. Now, his third "State of the City" speech is gaining unwanted attention from civil rights activists in the Democratic Party over his remarks given on March 11, 2015.

"There is no contradiction between respecting the risks that police officers take every day in order to protect this community, and recognizing the need to overcome the biases implicit in a justice system that treats people from different backgrounds differently, even when they are accused of the same offenses," Mayor Buttigieg said in mid-2015, when he adhered to the pro-police line, as the supervisor of his city's department. "We need to take both those things seriously, for the simple and profound reason that all lives matter."[50]

He has since "walked those comments back," in the parlance of political journalists, but the damage has been done in the minds of ordinary people who learn of the speech. As Daniel Victor of the *New York Times* explained, "the phrase 'all lives matter' is generally not seen as a Kumbaya sentiment, but as a way to remove focus from the specific grievances of black Americans."[51]

"The Mayor's comment was in the context of discussing racial reconciliation in his 2015 State of the City speech," said Lis Smith, a spokesperson for the Buttigieg campaign in a statement after those comments resurfaced. "He believes black lives matter and that has been reflected in his actions as mayor of South Bend."[52] His campaign's claim that it was taken out of context is not going to resonate well in the progressive base of the Democratic Party. It's very likely others will raise his comments in a negative light during the twelve Democratic primary debates.

FIGHTING INDIANA GOVERNOR MIKE PENCE'S FAILED ANTIGAY LAW

Mayor Pete had already received national attention for his innovative efforts by 2014, when the *Washington Post* called him "The Most Interesting Mayor You've Never Heard Of."[53] It turns out that the country would start hearing a lot about Buttigieg in 2015 because of a backbench Republican congressman who became Indiana's governor: Mike Pence. Yes, the same Mike Pence who is currently serving as vice president of the United States.

Then-Governor Pence signed into law a bill called the Religious Freedom Restoration Act (RFRA) on March 26, 2015. It extended religious expression to corporations in the wake of the Supreme Court's surprising *Hobby Lobby* decision interpreting the federal RFRA in an unintended way.[54] Despite its nice-sounding title, it was actually a bill to "protect Indiana citizens' right to practice their religious beliefs"—even if those beliefs meant practicing open anti-LGBTQ discrimination in Indiana business and public life.

Even though Indiana's discriminatory RFRA was only on the books in original form for a week, the AP reported that a study found the law cost the state's business community an estimated $60 million.[55] Compounding the problem for Pence and the Indiana GOP, who resoundingly passed the bill, the basketball-crazy Hoosier state was planning to host the National Collegiate Athletics Association (NCAA) Final Four championship tournament in Indianapolis's Lucas Center the following week.[56] Fifteen hundred journalists from around the country landed in the capitol, which also houses the NCAA's headquarters; the national college sports giant publicly contemplated pulling more events from Indiana that week. Apple CEO Tim Cook spoke out against the Republican-backed law, and Salesforce .com and Angie's List both canceled plans to expand in Indianapolis over the bill.

Three days after signing the Indiana RFRA, Gov. Pence went on ABC's Sunday-morning program, *This Week with George Stephanopoulos*, but he awkwardly refused to deny that the law's intent was to promote discrimination toward members of the LGBTQ community by businesses. Mayor Buttigieg made his first MSNBC appearance on the Reverend Al Sharpton's program *Politics Nation* just the following night at 6 p.m. Sharpton led the program with a clip of Stephanopoulos expertly pinning down the evasive Indiana governor, who looked like he was physically ready to flee the studio rather than answer a "yes or no" question:

> STEPHANOPOULOS: Yes or no question, Governor. Do you think it should be legal in the state of Indiana to discriminate against gays or lesbians?

> PENCE: George . . .

> STEPHANOPOULOS: It's a yes or no question.

PENCE: Hoosiers. . . . Come on. Hoosiers don't believe in discrimination.

STEPHANOPOULOS: Yes or no. Should it be legal to discriminate against gays and lesbians?

PENCE: George, you're following the mantra of the last week online . . .[57]

Mayor Pete wrote about his relationship with Pence in his book *Shortest Way Home.* Even though they were of different political parties, Buttigieg had gone out of his way to coordinate with the governor's office on a practical program to help all of their constituents.

Pence's plans changed the way local governments offer incentive plans to corporations to expand to Indiana. A patchwork of agencies used to line up to throw money at companies, reorganizing them by region to cut down on duplicate efforts and keep neighbors from literally competing with neighbors. The mayor spent a lot of time coordinating and participating in Pence's plan, which he described roughly as having been "set on fire" by the RFRA. He didn't hold back on MSNBC, starting by echoing Gov. Pence's remarks about "Hoosiers":

Well, when you're a mayor, you spend so much time and energy trying to attract businesses, trying to attract people to your community. Part of how you do that is you try to demonstrate that it's a 21st century community, that it's open to all. Look, we're all for religious freedom. I am. Everybody in South Bend is. But that doesn't mean it's OK to harm others in the name of religion. This is a bill that sends the exact wrong message about our communities and about our state.

And I wanted to get out there to let everybody know that this doesn't speak for all Hoosiers, this certainly doesn't speak for South Bend. We pride ourselves on being open to all.

I wish more communities in Indiana would follow South Bend's lead. I was proud, two years ago, to sign the human rights ordinance and it's something that protects—by the way, it also protects freedom of religion. But at the same time, it protects [LGBT] residents from discrimination. We need more of that.

And what's really troubling about this bill is it is aimed squarely at that local decision, which was the decision our community made. You know, I would expect conservative legislators and a conservative governor to be for local control, something that there's support for on both sides of the aisle. This is doing just the reverse and I just can't understand why anybody, especially when we're competing for people, we're competing for jobs, we're competing for conventions, why would anybody want to send the message that we're turning back the clock on equality?[58]

Mayor Buttigieg acquitted himself well on MSNBC with Sharpton and his point got across. But he didn't give any hints that he would return to the network's coverage very soon. Gov. Pence crumbled two days later, signing a bill on April 2, 2015, to explicitly protect the LGBT community from discrimination as part of the RFRA, nullifying its worst provisions. The damage was done.

COMING OUT

A month later, Pete Buttigieg won the Democratic primary for his office by an overwhelming margin against a single opponent with over 75 percent of the 10,774 ballots cast.[59] The following month, the mayor published an essay in the *South Bend Tribune*'s "Voices" section that would ultimately redefine him in ways both personal and political that resound to this day titled, "South Bend mayor: Why coming out matters." He wrote:

> *My high school in South Bend had nearly a thousand students. Statistically, that means that several dozen were gay or lesbian. Yet when I graduated in 2000, I had yet to encounter a single openly LGBT student there. That's far less likely to be the case now, as more students come to feel that their families and community will support and care for them no matter what. This is a tremendously positive development: young people who feel support and acceptance will be less likely to harm*

themselves, and more likely to step into adulthood with mature self-knowledge.

I was well into adulthood before I was prepared to acknowledge the simple fact that I am gay. It took years of struggle and growth for me to recognize that it's just a fact of life, like having brown hair, and part of who I am.

Putting something this personal on the pages of a newspaper does not come easy. We Midwesterners are instinctively private to begin with, and I'm not used to viewing this as anyone else's business. But it's clear to me that at a moment like this, being more open about it could do some good. For a local student struggling with her sexuality, it might be helpful for an openly gay mayor to send the message that her community will always have a place for her. And for a conservative resident from a different generation, whose unease with social change is partly rooted in the impression that he doesn't know anyone gay, perhaps a familiar face can be a reminder that we're all in this together as a community.[60]

It was a watershed moment for Pete Buttigieg personally. MSNBC covered the essay's release, noting that Indiana was already one of thirty-six states that permitted gay marriage.[61] The *Washington Post* updated its "most interesting mayor you've never heard of" report by saying that he took a "step forward" and that, "[Mayor] Buttigieg is on the path to becoming a symbol for change in a place that has previously resisted it."[62] Just ten days after publishing his essay, the U.S. Supreme Court issued a landmark ruling in *Obergefell v. Hodges* which found that the Constitution's 14th amendment demands equal protection under the law for same-sex couples to marry.[63]

Buttigieg's fateful column set off conflicting responses in his hometown newspaper, which published opinions letters ranging from "words both support and inspire Mayor Pete and help dispel the bias of a society that has stood in the way of progress far too long" to conservative religious ideology. "As a Christian and a resident of the city of South Bend, it deeply concerns me that our mayor seems to promote an environment that endorses homosexuality," wrote one resident, because he believes it's incompatible with his interpretation of the Bible.[64]

Less than four years later, Mayor Buttigieg joined Rachel Maddow in her MSNBC studio for a prime-time interview where she—the first out Rhodes Scholar from the United States—asked him about the most intimate details of his decision to come out. He said:

> First of all, it took me plenty of time to come out to myself. So, I did not the way you did or the way my husband did figure out at such an early age that—I probably should have. I mean, there are certain—plenty of indications by the time I was 15 or so that I could point, like, yes, this kid is gay. But I guess I just really needed to not be. You know, there's this war that breaks out I think inside a lot of people when they realize that they might

be something they are afraid of. And it took me a very long time to resolve that.

The city was a jealous bride for a long time and kept me busy. But it was really the deployment that put me over the top. I realized that you only get to be one person. You don't know how long you have on this earth. And by the time I came back, I realized, I got to—I got to do something.

Pointedly, the mayor came out during the midst of a reelection campaign that could've gone either way. "Back then I would have believed that you could either be gay or you could be married," he told a DC audience at the 2019 Victory Fund National Champagne Brunch about the reasons he waited so long to tell the public. "Not both. That if you were gay, you could either be out, or you could run for office."[65] As the mayor explained to Maddow, all he could do was take a leap of faith and count on his constituents to vote for him and for good government over political or religious ideology that might lead them to vote against him:

I mean, I felt like things were going well in the city. I felt like I had done a good job by the people of South Bend. I had some level of trust that I would be—that I would be rewarded for that with a reelection.

But there's no way to really know. There's no playbook. I mean, no executive in Indiana that had been out. And so, it was kind of a leap of faith. I just—I had—I wrote it all down, put it in an op-ed, dropped into the "South Bend Tribune" and saw what would happen.

South Bend voters reelected Mayor Buttigieg by a five-to-one margin over his Republican opponent. "I didn't think it would be possible to win with this kind of margin and I think it shows that the community is really united," Buttigieg remarked to local television station WNDU about capturing 80 percent of the vote.[66]

THE TRANSFORMATION OF DOWNTOWN SOUTH BEND

One of the major reasons that Mayor Buttigieg won over the voters of his city so overwhelmingly is that he brought a very specific vision of what South Bend should change. Specifically, his vision showed in his handling of the city's dilapidated downtown; from the moment he arrived, it required triage—especially the beleaguered Chase Tower, its tallest building. What has happened since then has been nothing short of transformational.

For starters, the mayor made a major change that opened up all of the other possibilities: replanning the city's streets to remove one-way roads drivers treated like highways and give right-of-way parity to bicycles in the process. His $25 million dollar "smart roads" program finished those improvements in 2017, alongside an array of traffic-calming measures and other programs.[67] Local business leaders report a new crowd of people spend time in downtown since the changes, and two major residential condo projects have begun in the area.[68]

South Bend's Chase Tower was in receivership when the mayor took office; there was only one prospective buyer with a clouded past, who, along with all of the building's stakeholders, was asking the city to invest over $5 million just to keep it running because the elevators were in disrepair.[69] The city's tallest building was on the brink of becoming a ghost tower when Buttigieg rejected that offer. Now, the tower has been transformed into a modern Aloft Hotel by Marriott.[70]

Another Buttigieg initiative is the redevelopment of the city's long-closed Studebaker auto factory into the Renaissance District.[71] A quirky happenstance of technology gives the old plant a significant advantage for high-traffic internet work; there is a lot of "dark fiber" or underutilized bandwidth from a cable from New York to Chicago running underneath it. "We sit on one of the richest concentrations of fiber-optic cable thruway in the country," Buttigieg told Public Radio International in 2017.[72]

Crucially for the city, its downtown tax base grew by 21 percent in value over the last six years.[73] Residents are weary that rents on the five hundred new downtown apartments are pricey and out of reach for many, and that's important in a city whose poverty rate is nearly double the national average. Still, it's a huge turnaround for a city that had to pour millions of dollars into tearing down hundreds of rotting houses each year to building new units, which exceeded the city's 2013 growth projections. Some people who grew up in South Bend are even starting to return, reports NPR, which is another sign that the city has turned the corner on its industrial past and has eyes to the future.[74]

RUNNING TO BE THE NEW CHAIRMAN OF THE DEMOCRATIC NATIONAL COMMITTEE

The mayor was busy implementing his vision for revitalizing South Bend throughout his second term, but a national columnist raised his profile substantially six months after his second swearing-in ceremony by writing a column titled with a provocative question: "The First Gay President?" Frank Bruni of the *New York Times* published that column in June 2016, from South Bend, about Mayor Buttigieg. He wrote:

> *Although voters in Wisconsin elevated an openly lesbian candidate, Tammy Baldwin, to the United States Senate, and Oregon's governor has described herself as bisexual, no openly gay, lesbian, or bisexual person has ever emerged as a plausible presidential candidate. How soon might that change? Could we look up a dozen or more years from now and see a same-sex couple in the White House?*
>
> *I'd wondered in the abstract, and after a veteran Democratic strategist pointed me toward Buttigieg as one of the party's brightest young stars, I wondered in the concrete.*
>
> *He probably winced when he read that: At no point during my visit with him last week did he express such a grand political ambition or define himself in terms of his sexual orientation.*
>
> *He seems always to say just the right thing, in just the right tone. When I asked why he signed up for the Navy*

Reserve, he cited his experience canvassing for Barack Obama in Iowa in 2008.

When I asked where the Democratic Party errs, he said that too many Democrats "are not yet comfortable working in a vocabulary of 'freedom.' Conservatives talk about freedom. They mean it. But they're often negligent about the extent to which things other than government make people unfree. And that is exactly why the things we talk about as Democrats matter," he continued. "You're not free if you have crushing medical debt. You're not free if you're being treated differently because of who you are. What has really affected my personal freedom more: the fact that I don't have the freedom to pollute a certain river, or the fact that for part of my adult life, I didn't have the freedom to marry somebody I was in love with? We're talking about deep, personal freedom."[75]

Six months later, Pete Buttigieg threw his hat in the ring for a run at the leadership of the entire Democratic Party, a serious run that, while unsuccessful, turned a lot of heads and introduced him to some of the key donors upon which he's relying for his 2020 primary run. After the 2016 election, the Democratic Party was in a state of shock and anger, and many people rushed to fill the leadership void, including South Bend's mayor. It is fairly easy to see in retrospect why he entered that long-shot race. A later *Politico* profile illustrated, for all to see, that the mayor had no clear upward path in public service in Indiana's political landscape, which is dominated by Republicans.[76]

"Many Democrats have expressed concern about reopening wounds from a presidential primary that highlighted their ideological, generational and racial fissures. Mr. Buttigieg supported Mrs. Clinton late in that race, but he is now casting himself as someone who can rise above the fierce internecine wars that linger from 2016, presenting himself as an alternative to a pair of Washington-based candidates," the *New York Times*'s Jonathan Martin wrote after he entered the race.[77]

Mayor Buttigieg deftly managed his media appearances during that run, and retained the same communications strategist for his primary run.[78] A search of Nexis reveals that the mayor was cited 530 times in national news stories about his DNC run. "What makes you different than Keith Ellison, the congressman, and Tom Perez, the labor secretary, because they're the two front-runners?" asked MSNBC's Chris Matthews when Buttigieg made one of his five appearances on the national cable news outlet during and after the race. "I'm 34 years old, but the best answer I have is my experience," said the mayor, inadvertently or maybe intentionally echoing one of his main 2020 primary campaign themes. "My experience is that of local governing, local politics. And at a time when we need to get, I think, back to the states and the communities, I just don't think the solutions for our party are going to come from Washington on down. And I think somebody who has that immediate, close-to-the-ground experience, not to mention being an executive, can really add something to the conversation here."

Three days before the DNC chairman vote took place on February 25, 2017, Buttigieg dropped bombshell news: former Vermont Governor and DNC Chairman Howard Dean endorsed his candidacy.[79] Dean has been a national figure since his insurgent 2004 Democratic primary run, which led to his fifty-states strategy to take back the House and presidency. Not only that, but he became the fifth former DNC chair to back Buttigieg's candidacy.

In the end, he gained the endorsements of two senators, a House Democrat from Indiana, dozens of other state and local officials, the VoteVets political action committee, and even the legendary singer Cher.[80] Unfortunately, that only translated into a single vote in the first round of balloting, which ended with former Rep. Keith Ellison (D-MN) in a run-off with the eventual winner, DNC Chairman Tom Perez.[81] "He wasn't running for DNC to be the end of it," said former DNC deputy executive director Moses Mercado to *Politico* in 2019 about the race.[82] "He wasn't running for DNC chair like: 'This is my dream. I wanted to be DNC chair and then retire. He wanted to inject himself in national politics."

Later that year, the mayor's increasing travel fell under granular scrutiny by the *South Bend Tribune*, which determined that he was spending nearly ten weeks per year out of town in 2016–17 versus only four weeks gone in his first two years.[83] It was hard not to notice that Buttigieg was hanging with a different crowd after Facebook founder Mark Zuckerberg dropped in for a livestream video chat in April 2017, during his plan to visit all fifty states that year.[84]

Mayor Pete used those opportunities to bring home innovative solutions. One example was the Los Angeles Mayor Eric Garcetti's decision to launch the national tech initiative Accelerator for America in South Bend after the two men met at a conference.[85] "I knew someday someone was going to write this story," Buttigieg told the *Tribune*'s city hall beat writer. "I've never taken a trip I wasn't prepared to defend or explain because my time is the one asset we can't get more of, so we're very intentional about how we budget it." Self-possessed actions like tracking his travel with an eye on preserving public integrity are a major sign of Mayor Buttigieg's fiscal discipline and ethics.

ANALYSIS OF PETE BUTTIGIEG'S CHANCES FOR WINNING THE NOMINATION AND PRESIDENCY

P ete Buttigieg launched his 2020 Democratic primary campaign with a high-energy campaign rally on a rainy April day in his beloved hometown of South Bend, Indiana on the floor of the old Studebaker factory that his mayoral administration turned into a tech incubator.[1] There was an overflow crowd. He began the race with an exploratory committee launching in January 2019 and remained at 1 percent in the polls, until breakout from the pack after a nationally televised CNN town hall event. Since then, he has remained in the top tier of a Democratic primary field that has ballooned to twenty-three contestants in May 2019; Buttigieg is averaging fifth in national polling, but crucially running third in early states Iowa *and* New Hampshire.[2] The South Bend mayor has become an early front-runner, raising a surprising $7 million, with 64 percent of it coming from small donors giving under $200. He has $6.4 million on hand at the end of the first quarter of 2019.[3] "We (you) are outperforming expectations at every turn," he wrote in a very Mayor Pete tweet promising more facts and figures.[4] "I'll have a more complete analysis later, but until then: a big thank you to all our supporters."

Buttigieg is staking his campaign on his preternatural political instincts, unique résumé and bio, and track record as a transformative city executive. He could struggle early on with the Democratic primary's proportional representation system, which only gives delegates to candidates who win more than 15 percent of the vote, because most of his polling figures stand under that number in the early-going of the campaign.

Mayor Buttigieg released a complete domestic agenda in mid-May 2019, but his foreign policy platform is thin. His personal memoir, *Shortest Way Home*, is a best seller and has more literary merit than as just a campaign bio; you know the candidate wrote it himself, because he's prone to quoting from it verbatim at times. He is rolling out his own flavor of Senator Bernie Sanders's signature "Medicare for All" initiative, which he calls "Medicare for all who want it," as a public health option. Recent polling from the nonprofit Kaiser Family Foundation finds that public support is very high to treat health care as a right, and Buttigieg said that his plan would not end private health insurance as we know it.[5] He also supports the Green New Deal proposed by Rep. Alexandria Ocasio-Cortez (D-NY) as an economic opportunity to create union jobs while fighting for millennial voters like himself.

"I think Mayor Pete's path to the Democratic nomination is questionable. He's got a lot of appeal and he's gotten a lot of attention," says Nolan McCaskill, who is traveling on the campaign trail and reporting on the 2020 Democratic primary candidates for *Politico*.[6] "But he does have one major flaw in his campaign right now, and that's that he is not reaching black voters . . . especially in an early state like South Carolina, they could lose a lot of momentum if he doesn't perform well there. I believe he can do well in Iowa. He can do well in New Hampshire."

"He served in Afghanistan. He's running for president as a married white man married to another white man, so he's running openly gay, which is a historic thing that I don't believe we've seen before in the Democratic primary," says McCaskill, recounting what is attracting so much "infatuation" with the mayor early in the race, in addition to his status as a newcomer. "He speaks a bunch of languages. He's a polyglot. He's gone viral on Twitter just for speaking another language and getting a bunch of attention and awing reporters, and that's kind of translated to voters as well. They're impressed. Everyone I talk to talks about how intelligent he is. They like his ideas. He's well-spoken. He's young." The *Politico* columnist mused that his own journalistic notes drove home the contrast between Biden and Buttigieg, when he realized that the former Delaware senator spent almost as much time in Congress as the mayor has been alive.

"I ran for mayor in 2011 knowing that nothing like Studebaker would ever come back—but believing that we would, our city would, if we had the courage to reimagine our future. And now, I can confidently say that South Bend is back," Buttigieg said at his campaign kickoff rally.[7] "More people are moving into South Bend than we've seen in a generation. Thousands of new jobs have been added in our area, and billions in investment. There's a long way for us to go. Life here is far from perfect. But we've changed our trajectory, and shown a path forward for communities like ours. . . ." He continued:

And that's why I'm here today. To tell a different story than "Make America Great Again." Because there is a myth being sold to industrial and rural communities: the myth that we can stop the clock and turn it back. It comes from people who think the only way to reach communities like ours is through resentment and nostalgia, selling an impossible promise of returning to a bygone era that was never as great as advertised to begin with. The problem is, they're telling us to look for greatness in all the wrong places. Because if there is one thing the city of South Bend has shown, it's that there is no such thing as an honest politics that revolves around the word "again."

It's time to walk away from the politics of the past, and toward something totally different. So that's why I'm here today, joining you to make a little news: My name is Pete Buttigieg. They call me Mayor Pete. I am a proud son of South Bend, Indiana. And I am running for president of the United States.

"My most immediate historic comparison for Mayor Pete would probably be Senator Bernie Sanders's 2016 campaign. I mean, these are two candidates who weren't really taken seriously when they launched their campaigns. They both surged," says McCaskill, who is a millennial himself—mostly from Washington, DC—that has covered politics since graduating from Florida A&M University at the end of 2014. "They both got a lot of attention out of national players, but they also both struggle courting black voters, and that could be their detriment. That problem could be what keeps Mayor Pete from ascending to the top ahead of Joe Biden and Bernie Sanders. It was what kept Bernie Sanders from really competing with Clinton all the way through that primary."

"South Carolina could be a very pivotal state," says McCaskill, who reported on the mayor's struggles to attract people of color on a May 2019 campaign swing there. "Right now Mayor Pete is polling at 0 percent among black voters, and polling alongside Senator Elizabeth Warren overall there." He described the mayor's South Carolina trip in *Politico*:

> Pete Buttigieg wants to have a conversation with African American voters. But he can't seem to reach them. He scheduled a meet-and-greet Monday in Orangeburg—a city that is 76 percent black—but only a dozen or so people of color showed up in a crowd of more than 100. At a town hall the night before—held at a North Charleston high school where minority enrollment is 97 percent in a city that is roughly half-black—it was another overwhelmingly white audience.
>
> "A lot of people don't know who he is on this side of the country or what he stands for," said state Rep. Jerry Govan, a veteran lawmaker who represents Orangeburg and chairs the state's Legislative Black Caucus. "The only thing people are getting about him is what they're seeing in national media."

At his event in Orangeburg, Buttigieg outlined his agenda for black America, an agenda that focuses on home ownership, health care, entrepreneurship, criminal justice reform and education. "One of the most import-ant pieces of homework for our campaign is to make sure that there is no question in the minds of any minority voters, black voters here in South Carolina or anywhere in the country, where I stand and what I will do," Buttigieg told the audience. He argues that minority voters who know him best, residents of South Bend, helped re-elect him mayor. "But out here, people are just getting to know me," he said. "Trust in part is a function of quantity of time, and we're racing against time."

McCaskill has also reported on the emanation of open frustration from some of Mayor Pete's similarly situated opponents, former mayors, who've got more national political experience but haven't yet gained media traction during the race.[8] Senator Booker is also a Rhodes Scholar and innovative former mayor of Newark, while former Cabinet Secretary Julián Castro is the former mayor of San Antonio, Texas, running a campaign to become the historic first Latino presidential nominee. "He's at a disadvantage anytime he's not treated on the same playing level as all the other candidates. There should be a campaign where people start to question the process when there's not fairness—and especially within the media," said South Carolina state Rep. John King, who has endorsed Booker to

McCaskill in a *Politico* story he wrote titled "'The epitome of privilege': Booker supporters seethe over Buttigieg mania."

"I think Mayor Pete is someone who has the best chance to really connect with younger voters because he is a young voter. He's the youngest candidate in the field," concluded McCaskill, who noted how the South Bend mayor has a big opportunity to flip the script on Republicans and entice Democrats frustrated with President Trump's political play to drive federal courts—and especially the Supreme Court—further to the right. He continued:

> Pete Buttigieg talks about on the campaign trail how he couldn't marry his husband if there wasn't that one vote on the Supreme Court legalizing gay marriage throughout the country. That was a vote that's relatively recent. It's not like something that happened in the 60s. And he's a product of that. He can speak to young voters about how issues on the Supreme Court affect people across the entire country, and the Supreme Court is an issue that Republicans used very well in 2016 to put Trump in the White House, and we've seen the effects of that as Trump continues to nominate conservative judges.
>
> Senate Majority Leader Mitch McConnell continues to push those judges through. And now we're seeing with some of these anti-abortion bills across different states that could end up being challenged in the Supreme

Court, abortion rights are sort of being chipped away across the country, and part of that stems from the fact that Republicans prioritize this issue, while Democrats really didn't make a big enough deal about it while Merrick Garland, President Barack Obama's nominee, was being held up in the Senate.

In the middle of May 2019, Buttigieg is placing fourth in half of the eight major national polls, which are tracked by *Real Clear Politics*, along with a third-place rating and the other three in fifth place.[9]

Since Buttigieg's poll numbers surged in March 2019, he is running solidly in third place in polling averages in both the early primary state of New Hampshire and the first caucus state, Iowa.[10, 11] A Suffolk University poll at the very end of April 2019 showed Mayor Pete in a statistical dead heat with Senator Sanders in New Hampshire.[12]

He is running third in the three major Iowa polls behind Biden and Sanders.[13] The Hawkeye state has to figure prominently into the mayor's election strategy. In many ways, his early campaign has ripped a page out of President Jimmy Carter's playbook. Carter was a little-known, one-term Georgia governor until he defeated an eleven-man field in Iowa in only their second early caucus, then leveraged that media coverage to elevate his profile until he defeated the rest of the field.[14] As if to underscore the parallels between the two men, President Carter recently invited Mayor Buttigieg to give a reading at his weekly Sunday Maranatha Baptist Church in Plains, Georgia, along with Chasten, his husband.[15] Two of his competitors for the nomination, Senator Booker (D-NJ) and Senator Amy

Klobuchar (D-MN), also have visited President Carter in similar fashion during the campaign.

Buttigieg didn't exceed the 1 percent mark in an April 1, 2019, poll released by the Harvard Institute of Politics—which he once led—which surveyed voters aged eighteen to twenty-nine. That poll named Senator Bernie Sanders as the most chosen candidate by a landslide.[16]

Early Wisconsin polling in March 2019 showed Senator Sanders was the clear leader and Harris placed fifth with 5 percent of the vote, but that primary contest is relatively late in the 2020 primary season and a lot has happened since that poll.[17] A poll conducted in Florida by Bendixen & Amandi showed that Senator Harris is in third place with 9 percent support as of March 2019, but trailing Biden by seventeen points and Sanders by just 2 percent.

Buttigieg polled in a tie for third in South Carolina with 10 percent of the projected vote, in an early May 2019 poll by the *Charleston Post and Courier*.[18] Conventional wisdom is that Pete Buttigieg will have to make a tremendous showing in South Carolina in 2020 if he wants to win the Democratic nomination, as well as winning a significant share of Iowa and New Hampshire's early primary delegates in order to propel him to victory on Super Tuesday, and throughout the entire heavy schedule of primaries set for March 2020.

Mayor Buttigieg's list of endorsements by mid-May only consists of a handful of mayors and state legislators around the country, including former DNC Chair Steve Grossman.[19] Cher's son Chaz Bono is a celeb supporter, as his mother was during the mayor's 2017 DNC chair campaign. And he received a surprising maximum individual donation from James

Murdoch, son of the founding owner of Fox News, who departed the conservative news outlet and family business after Disney purchased its non-news assets in the spring of 2019.[20]

The 2020 Democratic primary race is going to go on for thirteen months before the first votes are cast in New Hampshire's primary, sometime before February 11, 2020. Primary campaigns are dynamic by their nature, and most often the early front-runner does not capture the party's nomination.

A *Real Clear Politics* average of the polling for a head-to-head matchup between Donald Trump and Buttigieg shows the mayor winning narrowly, but the results vary wildly as of May 2019; Public Policy Polling shows a four-point margin in his favor, Emerson's poll shows a tie, and Fox News polling shows him losing by 1 percent.[21] A Quinnipiac poll in Pennsylvania showed Buttigieg leading Trump in a head-to-head matchup in that state by one point, while Joe Biden would win the theoretical matchup with Trump by a nine-point margin.[22]

Buttigieg has an objectively difficult path to becoming the Democratic nominee in 2020, but he has not had a difficult time distinguishing himself from a large field, many of whom will likely try to push him on matters of his mayoral track record and foreign policy details. He would have a tough road if he were to win a narrow plurality of pledged delegates, but not a majority going in to the Democratic National Convention, which would lead to a "brokered convention."[23] He's likely to be in the mix to be another candidate's running mate if he doesn't succeed in the primary, but might not fit on a ticket led by the two early front-runners, Biden and Sanders, both of whom would likely want to diversify their ticket if nominated. However, Indiana is a swing state that voted for President Obama in 2012, and the mayor's home region is a big part of that base who abandoned Democrats in 2016.

Pete Buttigieg can win the Democratic nomination, but he'll need to tackle his biggest political problems head-on, and maybe have a little luck, too. He would become the first gay person to earn a national party nomination for the presidency. Buttigieg's Midwestern appeal and his transformation of South Bend will provide the narrative of his campaign. His policy focus on domestic issues and fighting for intergenerational justice him a formidable candidate throughout the Democratic primary elections, and, if everything goes right, in the general election.

NOTES

INTRODUCTION TO PETE BUTTIGIEG

1. Parrott, Jeff. "South Bend Mayor Pete Buttigieg Vetoes Anti-abortion Group's Rezoning." *South Bend Tribune.* Last modified April 28, 2018. https://www.southbendtribune.com/news/local/south-bend-mayor-pete-buttigieg-vetoes-anti-abortion-group-s/article_0b08950f-cd02-5b15-93cf-ff3a29fa2515.html.

2. Johnson, Chris. "Pete Buttigieg Makes Pitch to LGBT Voters in Bid to Become First Out Gay President." *Washington Blade: Gay News, Politics, LGBT Rights.* Last modified February 8, 2019. https://www.washingtonblade.com/2019/02/05/pete-buttigieg-makes-pitch-to-lgbt-voters-in-bid-to-become-first-out-gay-president/.

3. Schneider, Elena, and Daniel Strauss. "'He's Disrupting the Entire 2020 Race': Buttigieg's $7M Haul Puts Dems on Notice." *Politico.* Last modified April 2, 2019. https://www.politico.com/story/2019/04/01/pete-buttigieg-2020-fundraising-1246916.

4. Wikipedia. "Endorsements in the 2020 Democratic Party Presidential Primaries." Last modified March 25, 2019. https://en.m.wikipedia.org/wiki/Endorsements_in_the_2020_Democratic_Party_presidential_primaries#Pete_Buttigieg.

5. Schwartz, Brian. "Pete Buttigieg to Attend 2020 Fundraiser Hosted by Broadway Mogul Jordan Roth." CNBC. Last modified March 27, 2019. https://www.cnbc.com/2019/03/26/pete-buttigieg-attending-broadway-mogul-jordan-roth-2020-fundraiser.html.

6. Lee, MJ. "Elizabeth Warren's New Promise: No Fundraisers, Phone Calls with Wealthy Donors." CNN. Last modified February 25, 2019. https://www.cnn.com/2019/02/25/politics/warren-fundraiser-promise/index.html.

7.   Murray, Stephanie. "Buttigieg Draws Huge Crowd at Northeastern U." *Politico.* Last modified April 3, 2019. https://www.politico.com/story /2019/04/03/pete-buttigieg-northeastern-university-1254963.

8.   Kristian, Bonnie. "Mandatory National Service Is a Terrible Idea." *The Week.* Last modified April 19, 2019. https://theweek.com/articles/835755 /mandatory-national-service-terrible-idea.

9.   Young, Alex. "Trump Likens Pete Buttigieg to Mad Magazine's Alfred E. Neuman." Yahoo. Last modified May 11, 2019. https://www.yahoo.com /entertainment/trump-likens-pete-buttigieg-mad-231012534.html.

10. Sikich, Chris. "Donald Trump Called Pete Buttigieg 'Alfred E. Neuman.' The Millennial Mayor Had to Google It." *Indianapolis Star.* Last modified May 11, 2019. https://www.indystar.com/story/news/politics/elections/2019 /05/11/alfred-e-neuman-pete-buttigieg-donald-trump-mad-magazine /1174609001/.

11. "A Fresh Start for America." *Pete For America.* Accessed May 17, 2019. https://peteforamerica.com/meet-pete/.

WHO IS PETE BUTTIGIEG?

1.   Cook, Tony, and Brian Eason. "Gov. Mike Pence Signs RFRA Fix." *Indianapolis Star.* Last modified April 1, 2015. https://www.indystar.com /story/news/politics/2015/04/01/indiana-rfra-deal-sets-limited-protections -for-lgbt/70766920/.

2.   "Hardcover Nonfiction Books - Best Sellers - March 3, 2019." *New York Times.* Last modified March 3, 2019. https://www.nytimes.com/books /best-sellers/2019/03/03/hardcover-nonfiction/.

3.   Martin, Jonathan. "Who's Running for President in 2020?" *New York Times.* Last modified May 2, 2019. https://www.nytimes.com/interactive /2019/us/politics/2020-presidential-candidates.html.

4.   Dovere, Edward-Isaac. "Mayor Buttigieg Is Working Remotely Today." *The Atlantic.* Last modified May 1, 2019. https://www.theatlantic.com/politics /archive/2019/05/buttigieg-road-south-bend/588427/.

5.   Quinnipiac University. "QU Poll Release Detail." Accessed May 6, 2019. https://poll.qu.edu/national/release-detail?ReleaseID=2617.

6. Wikipedia. "List of Presidents of the United States by Previous Experience." Accessed May 6, 2019. https://en.wikipedia.org/wiki/List_of_Presidents_of _the_United_States_by_previous_experience.

DEFINING MOMENTS IN PETE BUTTIGIEG'S POLITICAL CAREER

1. Struyk, Ryan. Twitter. Accessed May 6, 2019. https://twitter.com/ryanstruyk /status/1104549082893373441.

2. "Pete Buttigieg on Why He Wants to Face Off against President Trump in 2020 |The View." YouTube. January 31, 2019. https://www.youtube.com /watch?v=PI6IbymfkX8.

3. "Election 2020 - Iowa Democratic Presidential Caucus." *RealClearPolitics.* Accessed May 6, 2019. https://www.realclearpolitics.com/epolls/2020 /president/ia/iowa_democratic_presidential_caucus-6731.html#polls.

4. "Pete Buttigieg." Facebook. n.d. Accessed May 6, 2019. https://www .facebook.com/watch/?v=834805466869382.

5. Tapper, Jake. "CNN Hosts Town Hall with Mayor Pete Buttigieg." CNN. March 10, 2019.

6. French, Clifton. "Fact Check: Does Mayor Pete Have More Military Experience Than George W. Bush." ABC57. Accessed May 6, 2019. https:// www.abc57.com/news/fact-check-does-mayor-pete-have-more-military -experience-than-george-w-bush.

7. Rocha, Veronica, and Brian Ries. "CNN Hosts 2020 Town Hall at SXSW: Live Updates." CNN. Last modified March 11, 2019. https://www.cnn.com /politics/live-news/sxsw-town-hall-delaney-gabbard-buttigieg/index.html.

8. Daughtry, Leah D. Twitter. Accessed May 6, 2019. https://twitter.com /LeahDaughtry/status/1104923338965766144.

9. Lange, Kaitlin. "Mayor Pete Buttigieg Jumps in Google Searches, Claims Fundraising Spike Following CNN Town Hall." *Indianapolis Star.* Last modified March 12, 2019. https://www.indystar.com/story/news/politics /2019/03/12/mayor-pete-buttigieg-jumps-google-trends-following-cnn -town-hall/3139383002/.

10. Bradner, Eric. "Pete Buttigieg Makes Star Turn in Town Hall Spotlight." CNN. Last modified March 11, 2019. https://www.cnn.com/2019/03/11 /politics/pete-buttigieg-star-turn-cnn-town-hall-2020-democratic -presidential-race/index.html.

11. McKinnon, Mark. Twitter. Accessed May 6, 2019. https://twitter.com /mmckinnon/status/1104930359635005440.

12. Rubin, Jennifer. "Get ready for Pete Buttigieg." *Washington Post.* n.d. https://www.washingtonpost.com/opinions/2019/03/11/get-ready-buttigieg /?utm_term=.9aecbea0e02f.

13. D'Antonio, Michael. "Pete Buttigieg is the Human Rebuttal to Everything Mike Pence Stands for." CNN. Last modified March 12, 2019. https:// www.cnn.com/2019/03/12/opinions/pete-buttigieg-mike-pence-dantonio /index.html.

14. Merica, Dan. "Buttigieg Feels Momentum After CNN Town Hall, with $600K Raised in 24 Hours." CNN. Last modified March 12, 2019. https:// www.cnn.com/2019/03/11/politics/buttigieg-fundraising-townhall/index. html.

15. Stevens, Matt. "Who's in the Democratic Debates, and Who's in Danger of Missing Them." *New York Times.* Last modified April 30, 2019. https:// www.nytimes.com/interactive/2019/04/29/us/politics/democratic-primary -debates-2020.html.

16. Parnes, Amie. "Buttigieg Wins Stellar Reviews at CNN Town Hall." *The Hill.* Last modified April 23, 2019. https://thehill.com/homenews /campaign/433546-buttigieg-wins-stellar-reviews-at-cnn-town-hall.

POLICY: CAMPAIGN PLATFORMS

1. Darling, Kurt. "Freedom, Democracy, and Security: The Three Pillars Of Pete Buttigieg's Presidential Bid." 93.1 WIBC. Accessed May 17, 2019. https://www.wibc.com/news/local-news/freedom-democracy-and-security -three-pillars-pete-buttigiegs-presidential-bid.

2. Woolner, David. "FDR's Four Freedoms and Global Security." *Roosevelt Institute.* Last modified December 23, 2010. http://rooseveltinstitute.org /fdrs-four-freedoms-and-global-security/.

3. "A Fresh Start for America." *Pete For America.* Accessed May 17, 2019. https://peteforamerica.com/issues/.

4. Tapper, Jake. "CNN Town Hall with Mayor Pete Buttigieg." CNN. March 10, 2015.

5. Uhrmacher, Kevin, Kevin Schaul, Paulina Firozi, and Jeff Stein. "Where 2020 Democrats stand on Medicare-for-all." *Washington Post.* n.d. https://

www.washingtonpost.com/graphics/politics/policy-2020/medicare-for
-all/?noredirect=on&utm_term=.92cab7231939.

6.   "Hyde Amendment." Wikipedia. Last modified February 28, 2007. https://
en.wikipedia.org/wiki/Hyde_Amendment.

7.   Kenton, Will. "Lilly Ledbetter Fair Pay Act." Investopedia. Last modified
October 5, 2009. https://www.investopedia.com/terms/l/lilly-ledbetter-fair
-pay-act.asp.

8.   Johnson, Chris. "Pete Buttigieg Makes Pitch to LGBT Voters in Bid to
Become First Out Gay President." *Washington Blade.* Last modified February
8, 2019. https://www.washingtonblade.com/2019/02/05/pete-buttigieg
-makes-pitch-to-lgbt-voters-in-bid-to-become-first-out-gay-president/.

9.   Gardner, Drew. "South Bend Mayor Pete Buttigieg Weighs in on
Transgender Military Ban." ABC57. Accessed May 17, 2019. https://www
.abc57.com/news/south-bend-mayor-pete-buttigieg-weighs-in-on
-transgender-military-ban.

10. Doering, Jenni. "With Eyes on the Presidency, Mayor Pete Seeks a 'Generational Alliance' to Tackle Climate Change." Public Radio International.
Accessed May 17, 2019. https://www.pri.org/stories/2019-04-25/eyes
-presidency-mayor-pete-seeks-generational-alliance-tackle-climate-change.

11. Carbone, Christopher. "Pete Buttigieg Defends His Experience, Says 2020
Calls for Candidate with 'Completely Different' Background." Fox News.
Last modified March 29, 2019. https://www.foxnews.com/politics/pete
-buttigieg-defends-his-experience-says-2020-calls-for.

12. JTA, and Ron Kampeas. "Only Four Democratic Presidential Candidates
Weighed in on the Israel-Gaza Violence." *Haaretz.com.* Last modified May 7,
2019. https://www.haaretz.com/us-news/only-three-democratic-presidential
-candidates-weighed-in-on-the-israel-gaza-violence-1.7212567.

13. Buttigieg, Pete. "Why These Trump Voters Are Sticking Up For An
Undocumented Neighbor." *HuffPost.* Last modified March 21, 2017.
https://www.huffingtonpost.com/entry/why-these-trump-voters-are
-sticking-up-for-an-undocumented_us_58d14509e4b0e0d348b347e8.

14. Yarvin, Jessica. "What Does Pete Buttigieg Believe? Where the Candidate
Stands on 7 Issues." *PBS NewsHour.* Last modified February 15, 2019.
https://www.pbs.org/newshour/politics/what-does-pete-buttigieg-believe
-where-the-candidate-stands-on-7-issues.

15. Steinhauser, Paul. "Buttigieg Calls for Scrapping Death Penalty, Open to
Slavery Reparations." Fox News. Last modified April 4, 2019. https://www

.foxnews.com/politics/buttigieg-calls-for-scrapping-death-penalty-supporting
-slave-reparations.

16. "List of People Executed by the United States Federal Government."
     Wikipedia. Last modified June 5, 2016. https://en.wikipedia.org/wiki
     /List_of_people_executed_by_the_United_States_federal_government.

17. "Marijuana is No Longer a Fringe Issue for 2020 Presidential Candidates."
     Boston Globe. Accessed May 17, 2019. https://apps.bostonglobe.com/news
     /politics/graphics/2019/02/president-2020-candidates/issues-marijuana
     /#Buttigieg.

BACKGROUND AND EDUCATION

1.   Obituary for Joseph A. Buttigieg. Kaniewski Funeral Homes, Inc. Last
     modified January 28, 2019. https://www.kaniewski.com/notices/JosephA
     -Buttigieg.

2.   The University of Notre Dame. "Hesburgh-Yusko Scholars Program to Seek
     New Director to Replace Retiring Joseph Buttigieg." Notre Dame News.
     Accessed May 14, 2019. https://news.nd.edu/news/hesburgh-yusko-scholars
     -program-to-seek-new-director-to-replace-retiring-joseph-buttigieg/.

3.   Trebay, Guy. "Pete Buttigieg Might Be President Someday. He's Already
     Got the First Man." *New York Times.* Last modified January 24, 2019.
     https://www.nytimes.com/2018/06/18/fashion/weddings/mayor-peter
     -buttigieg-wedding-democratic-party.html.

4.   Parrot, Jeff. "Buttigieg wants to bring a fresh start to the city." *South Bend
     Tribune.* April 21, 2011. Accessed May 10, 2019 via Nexis.com.

5.   "2000 Winning Essay by Peter Buttigieg." John F. Kennedy Library.
     Accessed May 14, 2019. https://www.jfklibrary.org/learn/education/profile
     -in-courage-essay-contest/past-winning-essays/2000-winning-essay-by-peter
     -buttigieg.

6.   "Institute of Politics." *Wayback Machine.* Accessed May 14, 2019. https://
     web.archive.org/web/20130720160624/www.iop.harvard.edu/sites/default
     /files_new/011512_Iop_NL.pdf.

7.   Tapper, Jake. "CNN Town Hall with Pete Buttigieg." CNN. March 10,
     2019.

8. "The American Rhodes Scholar." *The Association of American Rhodes Scholars.* Accessed May 14, 2019. https://www.americanrhodes.org/assets/attachments/Scholars-Elect_2005_(TARS).pdf.

9. Joung, Madeleine M. "Fifteen Minutes with Mayor Pete." *The Harvard Crimson.* Accessed May 14, 2019. https://www.thecrimson.com/article/2019/4/11/mayor-pete-interview/.

10. "Rhodes Scholars Announced." *Harvard Gazette.* Last modified December 2, 2004. https://news.harvard.edu/gazette/story/2004/12/rhodes-scholars-announced-2/.

11. Father Edward Beck. "Pete Buttigieg on Faith, His Marriage and Mike Pence." CNN. Last modified April 2, 2019. https://www.cnn.com/2019/04/02/opinions/buttigieg-and-religion-qa-beck/index.html.

12. Bethea, Charles. "Deep Cuts from Pete Buttigieg's Rhodie Résumé." *The New Yorker.* Accessed May 14, 2019. https://www.newyorker.com/magazine/2019/05/13/deep-cuts-from-pete-buttigiegs-rhodie-resume.

13. Tapper, Jake. "CNN Town Hall with Pete Buttigieg." CNN. March 10, 2019.

14. Trumbull, Mark. "Obama: Detroit Auto Bailout Was Unpopular, but It Worked." *The Christian Science Monitor.* Last modified July 30, 2010. https://www.csmonitor.com/USA/Politics/2010/0730/Obama-Detroit-auto-bailout-was-unpopular-but-it-worked.

15. Adler, Leslie. "Chrysler Slams Indiana State Treasurer's Demands." *Reuters.* Last modified May 25, 2009. https://www.reuters.com/article/chrysler-indiana/update-1-chrysler-slams-indiana-state-treasurers-demands-idUSN2539345020090525.

16. Maureen Hayden CNHI Statehouse Bureau. "Indiana Treasurer Resumes Efforts to Intervene in Chrysler Bankruptcy Case." *Herald Bulletin.* Last modified April 14, 2010. https://www.heraldbulletin.com/news/local_news/indiana-treasurer-resumes-efforts-to-intervene-in-chrysler-bankruptcy-case/article_73d177c8-099e-5c78-8a6d-002e7fec8135.html.

17. Suddeath, Daniel. "State treasurer hopeful says Mourdock misjudged Chrysler case." *News and Tribune.* Last modified September 18, 2010. https://www.newsandtribune.com/archives/state-treasurer-hopeful-says-mourdock-misjudged-chrysler-case/article_ce9d4093-422e-5472-8428-f33e5a77bf20.html.

18. "Indiana - Election Results." *New York Times.* Accessed May 15, 2019. https://www.nytimes.com/elections/2010/results/indiana.html.

19. Davies, Tom. "Richard Lugar, Who Helped in Securing Soviet Arsenal, Dies." AP News. Last modified April 28, 2019. https://www.apnews.com /352a1bc4bc414a678a66abbd875fbba9.

20. Parrot, Jeff. "Who'll be city's next mayor?" *South Bend Tribune.* December 9, 2010. Accessed May 10, 2019 via Nexis.com.

21. Parrot, Jeff. "S.B. mayoral candidates talk jobs, houses." *South Bend Tribune.* March 11, 2010. Accessed May 10, 2019 via Nexis.com.

22. Parrot, Jeff. "Three South Bend mayoral hopefuls file finance reports." *South Bend Tribune.* December 9, 2010. Accessed May 10, 2019 via Nexis.com.

23. Ibid.

24. MAINSTREET. "America's Dying Cities." *Newsweek.* Accessed May 15, 2019. https://www.newsweek.com/americas-dying-cities-66873.

25. Buttigieg, Pete. "Voice of the People." *South Bend Tribune.* February 1, 2011. Accessed May 10, 2019 via Nexis.com.

26. Staff Report. "Briefs." *South Bend Tribune.* March 5, 2011. Accessed May 10, 2019 via Nexis.com.

27. Parrot, Jeff. "Chamber endorses Buttigieg for mayor." *South Bend Tribune.* April 1, 2011. Accessed May 10, 2019 via Nexis.com.

28. Colwell, Jack. "Field for S.B. mayor's race firming up." *South Bend Tribune.* April 3, 2011. Accessed May 10, 2019 via Nexis.com.

29. Parrot, Jeff. "Buttigieg has huge lead in campaign funds." *South Bend Tribune.* April 20, 2011. Accessed May 10, 2019 via Nexis.com.

30. Buttigieg, Pete. "He offers a plan for South Bend's economic growth." *South Bend Tribune.* April 21, 2011. Accessed May 10, 2019 via Nexis.com.

31. Editorial Board. "ENDORSEMENTS FOR MAYOR." *South Bend Tribune.* March 5, 2011. Accessed May 10, 2019 via Nexis.com.

32. "Śmigus-dyngus." Wikipedia. Last modified May 12, 2019. https://en .wikipedia.org/wiki/%C5%9Amigus-dyngus#South_Bend,_Indiana.

33. Colwell, Jack. "Dyngus Day and the campaign's final drive." *South Bend Tribune.* April 24, 2011. Accessed May 10, 2019 via Nexis.com.

34. "Briefs." *South Bend Tribune.* April 27, 2011. Accessed May 10, 2019 via Nexis.com.

35. Parrot, Jeff. "Dvorak ad attacks Buttigieg." *South Bend Tribune.* April 29, 2011. Accessed May 10, 2019 via Nexis.com.

36. "Briefs." *South Bend Tribune.* April 30, 2011. Accessed May 10, 2019 via Nexis.com.

37. Colwell, Jack. "The factors behind Buttigieg's big win." *South Bend Tribune.* May 8, 2011. Accessed May 10, 2019 via Nexis.com.

38. Laviola, Erin. "Pete Buttigieg's Campaign Staff: 5 Fast Facts." *Heavy.com.* Last modified March 25, 2019. https://heavy.com/news/2019/03/pete -buttigieg-campaign-staff/.

39. Colwell, Jack. "Negative campaign was a minus." *South Bend Tribune.* November 13, 2011. Accessed May 10, 2019 via Nexis.com.

40. Allen, Kevin. "Buttigieg, Wood win easily." *South Bend Tribune.* November 9, 2011. Accessed May 10, 2019 via Nexis.com.

41. Buttigieg, Pete. "South Bend will grow from a new groundwork." *South Bend Tribune.* December 26, 2011. Accessed May 10, 2019 via Nexis.com.

42. Parrott, Jeff. "James Mueller Rolls to Victory in South Bend Mayoral Primary." *South Bend Tribune.* Last modified May 8, 2019. https://www .southbendtribune.com/news/elections/james-mueller-rolls-to-victory-in -south-bend-mayoral-primary/article_4139cab3-c713-5d9c-be70 -7387ef7b806d.html.

MAYOR OF SOUTH BEND, INDIANA

1. "2011: A look back." *South Bend Tribune.* December 31, 2011. Accessed May 13, 2019 via Nexis.com.

2. "Unemployment Rate in South Bend-Mishawaka, IN-MI (MSA)." Federal Reserve Economic Data, St. Louis Fed. Last modified May 1, 2019. https:// fred.stlouisfed.org/series/SOUT718UR.

3. Lewis, Kevin. "SJC Records 21 Homicides in 2012, Higher Than Last Four Years." *WNDU 16.* Accessed May 17, 2019. http://www.wndu.com/home /headlines/SJC-records-21-homicides-in-2012-higher-than-last-four-years -182899261.html.

4. Allen, Kevin. "New year, new South Bend mayor." *South Bend Tribune.* December 31, 2011. Accessed May 13, 2019 via Nexis.com.

5. Moor, Bill. "Maybe this will be the year. . . ." *South Bend Tribune.* January 1, 2012. Accessed May 13, 2019 via Nexis.com.

6. Allen, Kevin. "Council gathers for first meeting." *South Bend Tribune.* January 3, 2012. Accessed May 13, 2019 via Nexis.com.

7. Ferreira, Colleen - WSTB reporter, "Buttigieg to propose pay raises for top staff." *South Bend Tribune.* January 5, 2012. Accessed May 13, 2019 via Nexis.com.

8. "A step forward." *South Bend Tribune.* March 29, 2012. Accessed May 13, 2019 via Nexis.com.

9. Allen, Kevin. "Debate stretches into night." *South Bend Tribune.* March 27, 2012. Accessed May 13, 2019 via Nexis.com.

10. Harrell, Jeff. "Crowd: 'We are Trayvon.'" *South Bend Tribune.* March 30, 2012. Accessed May 13, 2019 via Nexis.com.

11. Harrell, Jeff and Allen, Kevin. "South Bend Police Chief resigns." *South Bend Tribune.* March 30, 2012. Accessed May 13, 2019 via Nexis.com.

12. Gabriel, Trip, and Alexander Burns. "Pete Buttigieg Fired South Bend's Black Police Chief. It Still Stings." *New York Times.* Last modified May 13, 2019. https://www.nytimes.com/2019/04/19/us/politics/buttigieg-black -police-chief-fired.html.

13. The officers deny making any racist remarks.

14. Griffin, Drew. "Mayor Pete Buttigieg Addresses Demoting South Bend's First Black Police Chief Video." CNN. Last modified April 23, 2019. https://www.cnn.com/videos/politics/2019/04/23/pete-buttigieg-addresses -black-police-chief-ouster-griffin-dnt-tsr-vpx.cnn.

15. Easley, Jonathan. "Secret Tapes Linger over Buttigieg's Meteoric Rise." *The Hill.* Last modified April 15, 2019. https://thehill.com/homenews /campaign/438669-secret-tapes-linger-over-buttigiegs-meteoric-rise.

16. Sheckler, Christian. "After Negotiations Fail, South Bend Police Tapes Case to Drag on As Possible Trial Looms." *South Bend Tribune.* Last modified January 16, 2019. https://www.southbendtribune.com/news/publicsafety /after-negotiations-fail-south-bend-police-tapes-case-to-drag/article _21af3e28-e8b1-564c-a8a4-d4dac1f08703.html.

17. Griffin, Drew. "Mayor Pete Buttigieg Addresses Demoting South Bend's First Black Police Chief Video." CNN. Last modified April 23, 2019. https://www.cnn.com/videos/politics/2019/04/23/pete-buttigieg-addresses -black-police-chief-ouster-griffin-dnt-tsr-vpx.cnn.

18. Cooper, Anderson. "CNN Hosts Town Hall with Mayor Pete Buttigieg." CNN. April 22, 2019 air date.

19. Rowan, Nic. "Mayor Pete's 'First Serious Mistake'." *Washington Free Beacon.* Last modified April 2, 2019. https://freebeacon.com/politics/mayor-petes -first-serious-mistake/.

20. Griffin, Drew. "Mayor Pete Buttigieg Addresses Demoting South Bend's First Black Police Chief Video." CNN. Last modified April 23, 2019. https://www.cnn.com/videos/politics/2019/04/23/pete-buttigieg-addresses -black-police-chief-ouster-griffin-dnt-tsr-vpx.cnn.

21. "Executive Order 1-2016: Establishing a city-wide diversity and inclusion initiative." City of South Bend, Indiana. Accessed May 17, 2019. http:// docs.southbendin.gov/weblink/0/edoc/118239/Executive%20Order %201-2016%20Establishing%20a%20City-Wide%20Diversity%20and %20Inclusion%20Initiative.pdf.

22. Twardosz, Gina. "Officer of Diversity and Inclusion Focuses on South Bend Community." *South Bend Tribune.* Last modified December 17, 2018. https://www.southbendtribune.com/news/local/officer-of-diversity-and -inclusion-focuses-on-south-bend-community/article_0e802892-8ce9 -58e0-93df-7c5054ce7626.html.

23. Sheckler, Christian. "Fewer Crimes Reported in South Bend but Shootings Linger As Fears Remain for Some." *South Bend Tribune.* Last modified April 19, 2019. https://www.southbendtribune.com/news/local/fewer -crimes-reported-in-south-bend-but-shootings-linger-as/article_e6a6368d -5887-5131-8643-0dfdb21f278c.html.

24. Ibid.

25. "Giffords Law Center's Annual Gun Law Scorecard." *Giffords Law Center to Prevent Gun Violence.* Accessed May 17, 2019. https://lawcenter.giffords.org /scorecard/#IN.

26. Wood, Keith. "Best States for Gun Owners (2018)." *Guns and Ammo.* Last modified October 31, 2018. https://www.gunsandammo.com/editorial/best -states-for-gun-owners-2018/327233.

27. Schoen, John W. "States with Strict Gun Laws Have Fewer Firearms Deaths. Here's How Your State Stacks Up." CNBC. Last modified July 25, 2018. https://www.cnbc.com/2018/02/27/states-with-strict-gun-laws-have -fewer-firearms-deaths-heres-how-your-state-stacks-up.html.

28. "Here's a Look at the 30 Cities, Including 2 in Indiana, with the Highest Murder Rates in the U.S." *Nwitimes.com.* Last modified November 28, 2017. https://www.nwitimes.com/news/national/here-s-a-look-at-the-cities -including-in-indiana/collection_542dfcaa-f2ff-53bf-8e0a-fd36fa10fc60. html#30.

29. "South Bend Group Violence Intervention." City of South Bend. Accessed May 17, 2019. https://southbendin.gov/initiative/south-bend-group-violence -intervention/.

30. "Racial Wealth Divide in South Bend_ProsperityNow_Final_Rev.pdf." *Prosperity Now.* Accessed May 17, 2019. https://prosperitynow.org/sites /default/files/resources/Racial%20Wealth%20Divide%20in%20South %20Bend_ProsperityNow_Final_Rev.pdf.

31. "Vacant & Abandoned Properties Task Force Report." City of South Bend, Indiana. Accessed May 17, 2019. https://southbendin.gov/wp-content /uploads/2018/05/Code_FinalVATF_Report_2_red.pdf.

32. Land, Ted."A New Voice." WTSB. October 7, 2013. Accessed via YouTube: https://youtu.be/4vOyBn0vdBk.

33. Department of Housing and Urban Development. "South Bend's Vacant and Abandoned Housing Challenge: 1,000 Houses in 1,000 Days." Accessed May 17, 2019. https://www.huduser.gov/portal/pdredge/pdr-edge -inpractice-011116.html.

34. Buttigieg, Pete. "Vacant & Abandoned Properties Initiative." South Bend government website via the *Wayback Machine.* Accessed May 17, 2019. https://web.archive.org/web/20170207231010/https://www.southbendin .gov/sites/default/files/files/Code_VATF_ResidentInfoBook-032014.pdf.

35. Buttigieg, Pete. "Vacant & Abandoned Properties Initiative." City of South Bend, Indiana via *Wayback Machine.* May 17, 2019. https://web.archive.org /web/20180514192307/www.southbendin.gov:80/government/content /vacant-abandoned-properties-initiative.

36. "Vacant & Abandoned Properties: 1000 houses in 1000 days; community update." City of South Bend, Indiana. Accessed via *Wayback Machine.* May 17, 2019. https://web.archive.org/web/20161221185519/https://www .southbendin.gov/sites/default/files/files/dci/V%26A%20Community %20Update%20Presentation.pdf.

37. Mahaskey, Scott. "The President of Nowhere, USA." *Politico.* Last modified February 16, 2018. https://www.politico.com/magazine/story/2018/02/16 /pete-buttigieg-president-2020-profile-feature-217001.

38. Code for America. "Introducing CityVoice · Code for America Blog Archive." Last modified October 2, 2013. https://www.codeforamerica.org /blog/2013/10/02/introducing-cityvoice/.

39. Gomez, Henry J. "What Happened When Pete Buttigieg Tore Down Houses in Black And Hispanic South Bend." *BuzzFeed News.* Last modified

April 9, 2019. https://www.buzzfeednews.com/article/henrygomez/mayor-pete-buttigieg-south-bend-gentrification.

40. Sikich, Chris. "Pete Buttigieg Says He's Mayor of a Turnaround City. Here's How That Claim Stands Up." *Indianapolis Star.* Last modified March 21, 2019. https://www.indystar.com/story/news/politics/2019/03/21/pete-buttigieg-democratic-presidential-hopeful-south-bend-indiana-turnaround-city/3165477002/.

41. Bauer, Caleb. "South Bend Officials Highlight Home Repair Programs." *South Bend Tribune.* Last modified January 15, 2019. https://www.southbendtribune.com/news/local/south-bend-officials-highlight-home-repair-programs/article_f6cc225b-d89e-5bb0-9a17-7f6bff70255f.html.

42. "Pete Buttigieg Tried to Revive South Bend by Tearing Down Homes. Did It Work?" *The Christian Science Monitor.* Last modified April 5, 2019. https://www.csmonitor.com/USA/Politics/2019/0405/Pete-Buttigieg-tried-to-revive-South-Bend-by-tearing-down-homes.-Did-it-work.

43. Chronis, Kasey. "Goal of '1,000 Homes in 1,000 Days' Initiative Met." *WNDU 16.* Accessed May 17, 2019. https://www.wndu.com/home/headlines/South-Bend-celebrates-meeting-its-home-initiative-goal-328727261.html.

44. "Vacant & Abandoned Properties." City of South Bend. Accessed May 17, 2019. http://southbendin.gov/initiative/vacant-abandoned-properties/.

45. French, Clifton. "Fact Check: Does Mayor Pete Have More Military Experience than George W. Bush?" ABC57. Accessed May 17, 2019. https://www.abc57.com/news/fact-check-does-mayor-pete-have-more-military-experience-than-george-w-bush.

46. Wertz, Nathan. "Vets in Public Service: South Bend Mayor Pete Buttigieg." Military.com. Last modified October 16, 2018. https://www.military.com/undertheradar/2018/10/15/vets-public-service-south-bend-mayor-pete-buttigieg.html.

47. "M4 Carbine," Wikipedia. Last modified September 19, 2003. https://en.wikipedia.org/wiki/M4_carbine. Special thanks to Dr. James Eric McDonough for identifying the rifle.

48. Buttigieg, Pete. Twitter. Accessed May 17, 2019. https://twitter.com/petebuttigieg/status/743438113905713152?lang=en.

49. Blasko, Erin. "From South Bend to Afghanistan." *South Bend Tribune.* n.d. https://www.southbendtribune.com/news/politics/from-south-bend-to-afghanistan/article_376699a6-f9f2-11e3-b178-0017a43b2370.html.

50. Higgins, Tucker. "Democratic Hopeful Pete Buttigieg Addresses 'All Lives Matter' Controversy, Says He No Longer Uses the Phrase." CNBC. Last modified April 4, 2019. https://www.cnbc.com/2019/04/04/pete-buttigieg -addresses-all-lives-matter-controversy.html.

51. Victor, Daniel. "Why 'All Lives Matter' Is Such a Perilous Phrase." *New York Times.* Last modified December 21, 2017. https://www.nytimes.com /2016/07/16/us/all-lives-matter-black-lives-matter.html?module=inline.

52. Higgins, Tucker. "Rising Democratic Presidential Contender Pete Buttigieg Said 'All Lives Matter' in 2015, Putting His Record on Race in the Spotlight." CNBC. Last modified April 3, 2019. https://www.cnbc.com /2019/04/03/pete-buttigieg-on-police-controversy-said-all-lives-matter-in -2015.html.

53. Fuller, Jaime. "The most interesting mayor you've never heard of." *Washington Post.* n.d. https://www.washingtonpost.com/news/the-fix/wp /2014/03/10/the-most-interesting-mayor-youve-never-heard-of/?utm_term =.469772ca1641.

54. Stah, Shane. "Three Years Ago Today: Mike Pence Signed Indiana Religious Freedom Restoration Act Into Law." *Freedom for All Americans.* Last modified April 9, 2018. https://www.freedomforallamericans.org /three-years-ago-today-mike-pence-signed-indiana-religious-freedom -restoration-act-law/.

55. Slodysko, Brian. "Survey: Religious Objections Law Cost Millions." AP News. Last modified January 26, 2016. https://apnews.com /d79711fc58584c338d8e1002d80d66db.

56. "Religious Freedom Restoration Act (Indiana)." Wikipedia. Last modified March 26, 2015. https://en.wikipedia.org/wiki/ Religious_Freedom_Restoration_Act_(Indiana).

57. Stephanopoulos, George. *This Week.* Air date March 29, 2015. ABC.

58. Sharpton, Rev. Al. *Politics Nation.* Air date March 30, 2015. MSNBC.

59. Parrot, Jeff. "Pete Buttigieg rolls to victory in South Bend mayoral primary." *South Bend Tribune.* n.d. https://www.southbendtribune.com/news/local /pete-buttigieg-rolls-to-victory-in-south-bend-mayoral-primary/article _3f34cadb-633a-5e15-878f-bd09fd6d2b4e.html.

60. Buttigieg, Pete. "South Bend mayor: Why coming out matters." *South Bend Tribune.* n.d. https://www.southbendtribune.com/news/local/south-bend -mayor-why-coming-out-matters/article_4dce0d12-1415-11e5-83c0 -739eebd623ee.html.

61. Margolin, Emma. "South Bend, Indiana Mayor Pete Buttigieg Comes out As Gay." MSNBC. Last modified June 16, 2015. http://www.msnbc.com /msnbc/south-bend-indiana-mayor-pete-buttigieg-comes-out-gay.

62. Philips, Amber. "South Bend's mayor just came out as gay. Here's what you need to know." *Washington Post.* n.d. https://www.washingtonpost.com /news/the-fix/wp/2015/06/16/south-bends-mayor-just-came-out-as-gay -heres-what-you-need-to-know/.

63. Johnston, Maureen. "Obergefell V. Hodges." *SCOTUSblog.* Last modified November 18, 2014. https://www.scotusblog.com/case-files/cases/obergefell -v-hodges/.

64. Perri, Frank, and Powell, Charles. "LETTERS." *South Bend Tribune.* June 21, 2015.

65. Johnson, Chris. "Pete Buttigieg Engages LGBT Crowd by Sharing Personal Struggle of Being Gay." *Washington Blade.* Last modified April 8, 2019. https://www.washingtonblade.com/2019/04/07/buttigieg-engages-lgbt-crowd -by-sharing-personal-struggle-of-being-gay/.

66. Peterson, Mark. "South Bend Mayor Pete Buttigieg Wins Re-election." WNDU 16. Accessed May 17, 2019. https://www.wndu.com/home /headlines/Buttigieg-vies-for-second-term-as-South-Bend-mayor-340002362 .html.

67. Sisson, Patrick. "How Mayor Pete Used Good Urbanism to Revitalize South Bend." *Curbed.* Last modified April 14, 2019. https://www.curbed .com/2019/4/12/18308020/mayor-pete-buttigieg-president-development -urbanism.

68. Parrot, Jeff. "How much has Smart Streets driven downtown South Bend's turnaround?" *South Bend Tribune.* n.d. https://www.southbendtribune.com /news/local/how-much-has-smart-streets-driven-downtown-south-bend-s /article_493dc5c2-cd5a-5c17-ac8c-254c5362504b.html.

69. Allen, Kevin. "Future of Chase Tower remains in limbo." *South Bend Tribune.* February 28, 2012. Accessed May 16, 2019 via Nexis.com

70. Sikich, Chris. "Pete Buttigieg Says He's Mayor of a Turnaround City. Here's How That Claim Stands Up." *Indianapolis Star.* Last modified March 21, 2019. https://www.indystar.com/story/news/politics/2019/03/21/pete -buttigieg-democratic-presidential-hopeful-south-bend-indiana-turnaround -city/3165477002/.

71. Margolis, Jason. "After a Half-century, a Rust Belt Town Looks to Restore Its 'Temples'." Public Radio International. Accessed May 17, 2019. https://

www.pri.org/stories/2017-08-01/after-half-century-rust-belt-town-looks
-restore-its-temples.

72. Ibid.

73. Parrott, Jeff. "How Much Has Smart Streets Driven Downtown South
Bend's Turnaround?" *South Bend Tribune*. Last modified March 17, 2018.
https://www.southbendtribune.com/news/local/how-much-has-smart
-streets-driven-downtown-south-bend-s/article_493dc5c2-cd5a-5c17-ac8c
-254c5362504b.html.

74. Weingart, Jennifer. "Pete Buttigieg Helped Transform South Bend As
Mayor, But Some Feel Left Out." NPR.org. Last modified April 14, 2019.
https://www.npr.org/2019/04/14/712412977/pete-buttigieg-helped
-transform-south-bend-as-mayor-but-some-feel-left-out.

75. Bruni, Frank. "Opinion | The First Gay President?" *New York Times*. Last
modified December 21, 2017. https://www.nytimes.com/2016/06/12
/opinion/sunday/the-first-gay-president.html.

76. Mahaskey, Scott. "The President of Nowhere, USA." *Politico*. Last modified
February 16, 2018. https://www.politico.com/magazine/story/2018/02/16
/pete-buttigieg-president-2020-profile-feature-217001.

77. Martin, Jonathan. "Indiana Mayor Running for D.N.C. Chairman." *New
York Times*. Last modified January 20, 2018. https://www.nytimes.com
/2017/01/05/us/pete-buttigieg-democratic-national-committee-chairman
-race.html.

78. Strauss, Daniel. "Buttigieg's Bid for DNC Chair Ended with a Thud. Will
2020 Be Different?" *Politico*. Last modified April 23, 2019. https://www
.politico.com/story/2019/04/23/buttigieg-dnc-campaign-2020-1288768.

79. Weigel, David. "Howard Dean endorses dark-horse DNC candidate Pete
Buttigieg." *Washington Post*. n.d. https://www.washingtonpost.com/news
/powerpost/wp/2017/02/22/howard-dean-endorses-dark-horse-dnc
-candidate-pete-buttigieg/?utm_term=.f53385eea107.

80. "2017 Democratic National Committee Chairmanship Election."
Wikipedia. Last modified November 10, 2016. https://en.wikipedia.org
/wiki/2017_Democratic_National_Committee_chairmanship_election.

81. Ibid.

82. Strauss, Daniel. "Buttigieg's Bid for DNC Chair Ended with a Thud. Will
2020 Be Different?" *Politico*. Last modified April 23, 2019. https://www
.politico.com/story/2019/04/23/buttigieg-dnc-campaign-2020-1288768.

83. Parrott, Jeff. "A Jump in South Bend Mayor's Travels As His Star Rises Nationally." *South Bend Tribune*. Last modified March 27, 2018. https://www.southbendtribune.com/news/local/a-jump-in-south-bend-mayor-s-travels-as-his/article_c5e817d1-451b-5a16-a0f7-67c2f0714752.html.

84. Ryckaert, Vic. "Why Was Facebook CEO Mark Zuckerberg Hanging out with South Bend Mayor Pete Buttigieg and Elkhart Firefighters?" *Indianapolis Star*. Last modified May 1, 2017. https://www.indystar.com/story/news/2017/05/01/why-facebook-ceo-mark-zuckerberg-hanging-out-south-bend-mayor-pete-buttigieg-and-elkhart-firefighters/101145566/.

85. "Innovative Group Launches National Effort in South Bend." *Accelerator for America*. Accessed May 17, 2019. http://www.acceleratorforamerica.com/innovative-group-launches-national-effort-south-bend.

ANALYSIS OF PETE BUTTIGIEG'S CHANCES FOR WINNING THE NOMINATION AND PRESIDENCY

1. Merica, Dan. "Pete Buttigieg Officially Announces Presidential Campaign." CNN. Last modified April 15, 2019. https://www.cnn.com/2019/04/14/politics/pete-buttigieg-presidential-campaign/index.html.

2. "Election 2020 - 2020 Democratic Presidential Nomination." *RealClearPolitics*. Accessed May 17, 2019. https://www.realclearpolitics.com/epolls/2020/president/us/2020_democratic_presidential_nomination-6730.html#polls.

3. "Summary Data for Pete Buttigieg, 2020 Cycle." *OpenSecrets*. Accessed May 17, 2019. https://www.opensecrets.org/2020-presidential-race/candidate?id=N00044183.

4. Buttigieg, Pete. Twitter. Accessed May 17, 2019. https://twitter.com/petebuttigieg/status/1112648652781170694.

5. Beavers, David. "Buttigieg: 'Medicare for All' Wouldn't End Private Insurance." *Politico*. Last modified February 3, 2019. https://www.politico.com/story/2019/02/03/pete-buttigieg-medicare-for-all-1144293.

6. McCaskill, Nolan. Interview by Grant S. Stern. May, 17, 2019.

7. Burns, Alexander. "Pete Buttigieg's Campaign Kickoff: Full Speech, Annotated." *New York Times*. Last modified April 15, 2019. https://www.nytimes.com/2019/04/15/us/politics/pete-buttigieg-speech.html.

8. Mccaskill, Nolan. "'The Epitome of Privilege': Booker Supporters Seethe over Buttigieg Mania." *Politico*. Last modified May 13, 2019. https://www.politico.com/story/2019/05/13/cory-booker-pete-buttigieg-2020-1317660.

9. "Election 2020 - 2020 Democratic Presidential Nomination." *RealClearPolitics*. Accessed May 17, 2019. https://www.realclearpolitics.com/epolls/2020/president/us/2020_democratic_presidential_nomination-6730.html#polls.

10. Sparks, Grace. "New Poll: Buttigieg Surges into Top Tier in New Hampshire." CNN. Last modified April 23, 2019. https://www.cnn.com/2019/04/22/politics/unh-poll-march-buttigieg-biden-sanders/index.html.

11. Cadelago, Christopher. "New Hampshire Gives Harris a Hard Time for Rarely Showing Up." *Politico*. Last modified February 19, 2019. https://www.politico.com/story/2019/02/19/new-hampshire-kamala-harris-1173820.

12. Steinhauser, Paul. "Pete Buttigieg Tied for 2nd in New Hampshire Poll." Fox News. Last modified April 30, 2019. https://www.foxnews.com/politics/buttigieg-ties-sanders-for-second-new-hampshire.

13. "Election 2020 - Iowa Democratic Presidential Caucus." *RealClearPolitics*. Accessed May 17, 2019. https://www.realclearpolitics.com/epolls/2020/president/ia/iowa_democratic_presidential_caucus-6731.html.

14. Zelizer, Julian E. "How Jimmy Carter Revolutionized the Iowa Caucuses." *The Atlantic*. Last modified January 25, 2016. https://www.theatlantic.com/politics/archive/2016/01/jimmy-carter-iowa-caucuses/426729/.

15. Reeves, Jay. "Buttigieg, Husband Attend Jimmy Carter's Sunday School Class." AP News. Last modified May 5, 2019. https://apnews.com/503b9ce765f84205849b7af3540fbd7a.

16. Rodrigo, Chris M. "Sanders Leads Poll of Young Democrats by Double Digits." *The Hill*. Last modified April 1, 2019. https://thehill.com/homenews/campaign/436675-sanders-leads-poll-of-young-democratic-voters-by-double-digits.

17. Emerson Polling. "Wisconsin 2020: Bernie Sanders Leads Democratic Field; Trump Competitive in General Election." Accessed May 17, 2019. https://emersonpolling.reportablenews.com/pr/wisconsin-2020-bernie-sanders-leads-democratic-field-trump-competitive-in-general-election.

18. Shain, Andy. "'The Safe Choice:' Biden Widens SC Lead in 2020 Democratic Presidential Primary." *Post and Courier*. Last modified May 13,

2019. https://www.postandcourier.com/politics/the-safe-choice-biden
-widens-sc-lead-in-democratic-presidential/article_f727895c-731f-11e9
-888a-af4280777b2a.html.

19. "Endorsements in the 2020 Democratic Party Presidential Primaries."
Wikipedia. Last modified March 25, 2019. https://en.wikipedia.org/wiki
/Endorsements_in_the_2020_Democratic_Party_presidential_primaries
#Pete_Buttigieg.

20. Sobel, Barbara. "Pete Buttigieg Gets Support From a Kennedy, Celebrities,
and Conservatives." *Guardian Liberty Voice.* Last modified April 15, 2019.
https://guardianlv.com/2019/04/pete-buttigieg-gets-support-from-a-kennedy
-celebrities-and-conservatives/. Author's note: Confirmed by FEC records
search May 17, 2019.

21. "Election 2020 - General Election: Trump Vs. Buttigieg." *RealClearPolitics.*
Accessed May 17, 2019. https://www.realclearpolitics.com/epolls/2020
/president/us/general_election_trump_vs_buttigieg-6872.html.

22. Quinnipiac University. "QU Poll Release Detail." Accessed May 17, 2019.
https://poll.qu.edu/pennsylvania/release-detail?ReleaseID=2620.

23. Allen, Jonathan. "Why the 2020 Democratic Primary Could Turn into
'Lord of the Flies'." NBC News. Last modified January 24, 2019. https://
www.nbcnews.com/politics/2020-election/why-2020-democratic-primary
-could-turn-lord-flies-n961236.